MISTAKEN IDENTITIES

James Robertson was born in 1958 and grew up in Bridge of Allan, Stirlingshire, where his chief occupation was writing teenage Westerns. He studied history at Edinburgh University, later returning to complete a doctorate on Walter Scott. He has lived in the USA and Australia and has worked at different times as a lion keeper, pen pusher, ice packer, fruit picker, gold digger, mud slinger, van driver and bookseller. As holder of the Brownsbank Writing Fellowship he has been involved with writers' groups throughout Clydesdale, as well as working in schools and social work centres. He is the author of two collections of short stories, *Close* (1991) and *The Ragged Man's Complaint* (1993). While based at Brownsbank he has also prepared new editions of *My Schools and Schoolmasters* and *Scenes and Legends of the North of Scotland* by the Cromarty stonemason Hugh Miller (1802-1856), and edited a collection of contemporary short stories written in Scots, *A Tongue In Yer Heid* (1994).

Brownsbank Cottage, for nearly thirty years the home of Hugh MacDiarmid, is now owned and cared for by Biggar Museum Trust. It has been preserved as it was when the poet and his wife Valda stayed there, and can be visited by appointment through the Museum at Moat Park, Biggar.

MISTAKEN IDENTITIES

Edited by James Robertson

He builds his poems from old stones,
Lupins, butterflies, bric-a-brac and guilt.
Each one in turn an accomplice and an alibi.

BIGGAR MUSEUM TRUST
1994

First published 1994
by Biggar Museum Trust
Introduction and selection © James Robertson 1994
Contents © the Contributors
ISBN 0 95201451 3

CONTENTS

Introduction

Poetry might be defined as the art of saying the unsayable, fiction as the arrangement of a series of lies to create a truth. But with a little imagination you can easily swap these definitions around. Poetry and fiction are not really that far removed from one another, in spite of the barrier that is often erected between them. A good poem tells a story, although not necessarily in a conventional way: it accumulates images, fits words together to create a movement between the first and last lines: something *happens*. On the other hand a good story will have something poetic about it: through the creative use of language it will do more than just narrate a succession of events one after the other. If there is an idea unifying the poems and stories of these fifteen writers from Clydesdale, it is this: how you say something is at least as important as what you say. After all, there is nothing under the sun that hasn't been said in some way before.

You may start with what looks like a fairy tale and find, in Grace Sim's three variations on the traditional form, some unsettling possibilities creeping through the woods. Or you may look for stereotypes in Ethyl Smith's story of sudden illness and the different responses to it and find that the shifting angle of the narrative undermines your expectations. In other stories there's a subtle interplay between memory and observation, between the "real" and "imagined" experiences of the writers which combine to create sensitive, humane and moving portraits of people at moments of change: Agnes Thomson's child Beth running from a "half-remembered, old man smell"; G.C. Bryson's young man seeing his own emptiness reflected in the face of a much older man; Tom Crowe's portrait of a woman in the throes of depression.

This last story, "Alone", uses a slightly unconventional narrative technique to bring home the sense of despair to an intrusive "audience" of readers. In "Posha" by Nancy Yuille, the split perspective of the narrative produces an understated but compelling sense of fear and guilt between both generations and races: the power of this story lies as much in what is left unsaid as in its simple, unpretentious observation. And then there are the stories by Ian Hunter and Robert Hume—one a kind of horror story of the present (with a nice sense of irony in its advice to would-be authors), the other describing a future society where internal authority and external dangers seem similarly menacing. In both, imagination is used freely to make us question our assumptions about the world we think we live in.

Like Nancy Yuille's "Posha", Murray Davidson's rolling, rhythmic celebration of the mango is set in Africa. This is a long poem, which contains scenes of heat, flies, thieves and the succulent fruit itself as vivid as in any piece of fiction. It's good that so much of the work here bursts out of the local, but it's also good that, in some of the other poems, landscape and locality play an important part in the shaping of thoughts: after all, what is local to one person is exotic to a stranger. And there is something *outlandish* about Robert Hume's "segs of mud/Gouted from the tyres' dinosaur tread", or his clouds that are "cold grey duvets slowly tucking down". Eileen Whitelaw's gentle images of nature are accurately observed but hold their surprises: it would be hard to improve on a line like "The warm blue summer falls like silk". And in Douglas Robertson's intense use of colour and his interest in the lay-out of words against the page, the mind of a painter is instantly revealed.

Elsewhere, some of the writers here concentrate on relationships, social or anti-social behaviour, hope and futility in people's daily existence. Rosalinda Dawson uses unlikely incidents in mundane lives, or symbols like a doll or the three wise monkeys, to comment on the passing of time, the constraints of family, guilt, or responsibility on an individual's freedom of choice. Marilyn Scanlan's poems are often about relations between men and women, but she sees them from unusual angles, able to mix hurt and rage with a certain fatalistic humour too. Likewise there is humour and also anger in Ian Hunter's four poems, snapshots of life from his "Happy Baby" to the terrible dying of "Not Like That". Meanwhile William-John Deerin's poems range right across landscape and emotion, past and present, with a seriousness of purpose that is reflected in his careful structuring of rhyme and verse-form. Perhaps Paul Dawson's poetry is the most experimental and "difficult" in the book. It challenges the reader to search for meanings, demonstrating what any anthology of writing reveals: there are more ways than one to interpret the world.

The focus for assembling this anthology (which grew out of submissions from some forty writers) has been the former home of Hugh MacDiarmid, Brownsbank Cottage near Biggar, where I have held the post of Writer-in-Residence. MacDiarmid was a great believer in the constructive relationship between the local and the universal. Echoing that belief, I would conclude by saying that, while this book is diverse and far-reaching and deserves to be read outwith the confines of any administrative boundary, I hope the people of Clydesdale will take some satisfaction and maybe a little pride from seeing it in print.

James Robertson
Brownsbank
August 1994

Thanks to:

Biggar Museum Trust, for permission to use
the photograph from the Reverend George Allan
Collection for the design of the cover.

Clydesdale District Council and the Clydesdale Writers
Group for financial assistance towards publication.

Steven Wiggins and Campbell Brown, for professional
advice on typesetting and cover design.

POSHA

Nancy Yuille

The child looked down at her Wellington boots. Her toes
felt hot and sticky and the rubber seemed to be melting into
her skin. She wished that she could take them off and run
barefoot over the baked, fissured earth, but she knew that
the boots must stay on, in case of scorpions or snakes. The
child knew also that she must never point her toy gun at
anyone, not even in a game. And she knew how to get to
Aunt Pearl's house. It was just across the park and through
the fence. She could see it from here, and that was where she
was going. The hot rubber boots slapped her calves as she
marched purposefully along and she looked back just once
at her own house. Her mother was not within sight.

The cool dimness inside the house was like a blessing.
The child inhaled the scent of ebony wood and blossoms
and Aunt Pearl. She wandered to the accustomed room,
where there were small desks and chairs, and sat down to
wait. Soon, she heard Aunt Pearl's approach, the thud of
her stick on the polished wood floor and the whisper of her
slippered feet. The child jumped up to greet her, but
something in the old woman's demeanour halted the
impulse. Aunt Pearl passed the child without seeing her
there, the skin of her aged face shining with heavily-
fragranced moisturising oil. The child looked to the half-
open door of the room from which the old woman had
come. She had not seen inside this room: she walked to the
door and put her head inside. The shades on the windows

were drawn and the child's eyes took a moment to become accustomed to the semi-darkness. She opened the door a little wider. There was a great high table, set with glasses and dishes and candlesticks, and two rows of chairs were drawn up to the table. There was a baby highchair too. But something was wrong. She frowned and took a step backward. A cool hand fell on her shoulder, and the child looked up into the face of Aunt Pearl's manservant, who shook his head at her and closed the door of the room.

Aunt Pearl smiled when she saw the child, and made her sit down and sent for lemonade and cakes. Then she sat quietly, with her eyes almost closed, and did not offer conversation or a story, as was her custom. Soon, feeling awkward, the child stood and thanked the old woman, then turned and trotted through the cool house and out again into the brilliance of the day.

In the shade the men were squatting, sharing food from a large bowl. They ate with their fingers, somehow effortlessly elegant, and made mysterious conversation. The child squatted with the men. One of them was Aunt Pearl's manservant. They grinned at her, their teeth dazzling white, and one of them laughed a little. Then they offered her some food, called posha, and carried on their conversation. The child ate the bland porridge and sat watching the men, listening to the cadences of their speech, aware of their scent.

The woman stood for a moment, leaning by the sink in the tiled coolness of the kitchen. Her daughter was outside, playing under the jacaranda on a swing. Sometimes there was a sunshower, and the blue and purple jacaranda blossoms would come down with the rain and lie in deep fragrant drifts beneath the trees. The woman wished for a shower, to break the heat. Everything seemed so much harder to bear in the middle of the day with the sun hammering down. She would go out and call her daughter in a few minutes, when she had finished preparing the midday meal. She must speak to the child, and explain to her about the danger. She had shrunk from this until now, feeling that the child was too young to be burdened and frightened by reality. And there had been no local trouble until last night. The Mau-Mau was over, but still there were sporadic incidents, which was why they were here. British soldiers had been posted in Nairobi for some years. Their children went to school in troop-carriers, with an armed guard.

Whenever she thought of the Mau-Mau, she thought also of Pearl, the old widowed lady across the park. All of her family, even the children, slaughtered like animals, while on their way to visit Pearl. It was said that the dinner table was still set, as if they were still expected, although it was almost a year now. And the old woman kept her house staff, because she was frail and they had been faithful to her, and they stayed knowing of the retribution that had been meted out to others who served the whites. The woman sighed, thinking of how her daughter would cry when told that she must not visit Aunt Pearl alone again, and why, but it was too much of a risk to take. There were men in the area now, strangers, and the woman was afraid after last night, when only a few miles away there had been a robbery and killing of a white man. To think that Pearl had taught the native children for so long and had lived her life in this country, only to come to this in her last years, a time of fear and betrayal.

Suddenly aware of the quietness, the woman walked to the open French windows. The swing hung motionless in

3

the still heat. The child was not there. The woman ran outside and turned full circle, scanning. Her neighbour's children were already inside, out of the heat. She called the child's name. The stillness seemed to absorb the sound of her voice. Then the woman looked across the park, and knew. She began to run, panic tight in her throat. It seemed to take an age to reach the fence and then she ducked through it in one movement and hurtled around the corner of the house into the clearing, and saw the child immediately. She stopped, her legs weak with relief. Then she walked to the circle of men, feeling suddenly vulnerable under their stare, instinctively reaching to close the neck of her blouse. She took the child's arm, drew her to her feet. She tried to smile, and looked at their faces. She knew most of these men, and did not miss the reproach in their eyes. She nodded to them and turned away, the child's slender wrist soft in her hand.

POEMS

Rosalinda Dawson

BOLD TYPE

I *Press the Correct Key*

I know of a man
who went out one morning
to buy a newspaper
and who didn't return
till two years later.
I also know a woman
who went out to buy
a bottle of milk
but came back
with a car.
Sounds like a painting
by Magritte,
but gestures like these
amuse and amaze me.
They also set me
thinking.
Is it possible
to re-programme a brain
to behave
out of character?

II *Caps Lock*

Yesterday I bought a hat.
Not an ordinary, cover-your-ears
keep-your-head-warm hat;

but an elegant, black silk affair,
to wear at a wedding.
In the past I have watched impersonators
create different characters
merely by changing hats and voices,
and I thought the transformation clever.
But as I paraded before the glass
wearing the grand chapeau,
I suddenly realised how simple
it could be to exchange
one role for another.

III *Shift*

He stroked my neck.
That amounts to a pass.
No man has made a pass
at me for years—more years
than I can remember.
I have an icy,
"dare-you" stare
that nips all freshness
neatly in the bud.
But he caught me
without the mask,
fear-driven into
a corner.
He saw his advantage
and took his chance.
"DON'T!" I said.
He backed off
like a child chastised.
"Why not?" he asked.
And I catch myself
wondering.

THREE MONKEYS

Face like a painted Gesù,
and wrapped up in music
to the exclusion of all else,
my brother sheds responsibility
like dry skin.

Strong and silent,
finding a path around
the emotional debris
of family and financial ruin,
my sister gathers all problems
and hugs them to herself.

I withdraw;
refusing to see
what is obvious to everyone;
that as long as I remain where I am,
I will never find peace.

And the organ-grinder plays
as we dance through life,
each held fast
by the constraining leash.

DOLL

I'm holding myself together
like an old, worn Pierrot doll.
Sometimes stitches work loose
and I repair them.
For a while I was
coming apart at the seams,
but I've always been good
with a needle,
invisible mending is a
speciality.
That last time, for the
first time, the stuffing
came out.
Everyone could see it,
old and dirty.
I pushed it back;
drew raw edges together
neatly, expertly.
And looking at it
you would never know.
But like anything that's been
repaired, it needs
careful handling.
It's fragile where it's been broken;
will always have a weak spot.
However, I could sit it
on the shelf.
Left alone,
it would last for years.

8

HAIKU YEAR

Winter

Illness depresses,
A weakness that saps the brain.
I long for the sun.

Spring

New life all around,
Promise of many delights.
I hope for rebirth.

Summer

Lazy days of heat.
I doze among the flowers,
Make plans in secret.

Autumn

Season of harvests;
A gathering of produce.
I reap the rewards.

THE OUTING

G.C. Bryson

Dave decided quite quickly that he did not like Thorpley-by-the-Sea. Not that there was any reason why he should, but Joan's sentimental attachment to the place made him feel slightly guilty. The weather didn't help—it was a damp, gusty east-coast day, with a cold wet sea-mist hanging over the beach. Ha! thought Dave, that's no beach, that's mud-flats, that is. Turning his back to the wind, he gazed gloomily over the rows of dingy boarding-houses that stretched along the sea-front. The town, like an old and rather disreputable lady, smiled archly and anciently through the hanging veils of mist. Well, he thought, all we need is a fun-fair. A change of wind brought the sound of jangly, thumping music to his ears. There *was* a fun-fair.

Joan, however, had the quiet, withdrawn air of the dreamer, and in her dream she saw herself in a time when it was always summer . . . a little girl running barefoot in the warm sand, her long blonde plaits bouncing on her back, her frock tucked up into the legs of her knickers, heading pell-mell for the sea. She could see her beloved father watching her splash and scream in the sun-warmed waves. This was their escape from the grimy streets of the neighbouring town, and, before returning to them, just to ease the pain of departure a little, they would cross the road to the little cafe in Oswald Street. The cafe meant lemonade and cake, tall wooden chairs to scramble up upon, and marble-top tables that were cool on hot bare arms. The childish sunlight of those past years filtered through Joan's dreaming and shone in her eyes.

Dave studied her surreptitiously and was surprised. He hadn't realised what this place meant to her. And looking at it, who could blame me, he thought. Joan suddenly became aware of his scrutiny and, as their eyes met, Dave was not quite quick enough to hide the fact that he was cold, wet and restless. She laughed at him.

"I know what you're thinking! Let's go for a coffee, then we'll leave, all right?"

"Fine by me," he said. "But look, love, I don't want to rush you. It's just that other people's memories don't keep the wind and rain out. I'm frozen." The wind threw more cold salty raindrops at them as they crossed the road to Oswald Street.

Brown paint, wood and marble had given way to smart pastel shades and chrome and plastic laminates, but Joan could still see the window where the little blonde girl and her father used to sit. The cafe was deserted. A young girl with frizzy wire-wool hair and greasy make-up stood behind the counter, watching them without apparent interest. Dave ordered two coffees and they went and sat at the window table.

"I'm sorry to drag you out here, Dave . . ." Joan began. Dave waved a hand at her.

"Don't worry about that. What I want to know is—has it been a mistake for you? You know what they say about coming back. Should you have left well alone?"

She didn't answer immediately. Looking out of the window, she could see shops with all the usual hallmarks of the seaside town—the tatty souvenirs, the beach toys, the postcards. Now she could remember her parents wandering along there, her father with an open-necked shirt,

11

his jacket folded neatly over his arm, her mother in a fresh cotton summer dress. They would window-shop while she, full of impatience as she heard the cries of the other children on the beach, tugged at their hands. She turned back to Dave.

"No. It was right to come back. I had such a lovely childhood down here, Dave, but since my folks died some of it seemed to die with them. I didn't want to lose it, let it just slip away like a dream. I needed something to hang on to—to see the beach and the sea and the shops . . . and the cafe!" She laughed. "Drink your coffee and cheer up, for goodness' sake!"

But Dave was thinking how good it must be to have these warm happy memories. Good for the soul, he thought. He checked his own store of childhood memories. Days at the seaside? Nope. Lemonade and ice-cream in cafes? Nope. Loving tender care from parents? . . . It hadn't really occurred to him before, that he just seemed to have a black hole where the memories ought to be. Christ, he thought angrily, everyone should have something to look back to— something good, something nice. His childhood suddenly seemed as grey, sullen and featureless as that sea outside. He was surprised at how angry he was. All this time he had had this deep quiet anger inside him, so deep and so close that he himself had hardly been aware of it. Maybe I've just forgotten the good times, he thought. But another part of his mind answered him. No one forgets the good times, Dave. Better check out your soul.

They had almost finished their coffee when the door opened and a woman called out, "This way, this way! In we go! That's right. Just sit at any table—any one at all. Come along everyone!" Her voice was alternately cajoling and peremptory.

12

"It's an outing," murmured Joan, "an old folk's outing."

A little tide of ancient humanity spilled hesitantly between the tables, led by two very old ladies who were supporting each other and who had some difficulty in deciding which table to take, and then which chairs to sit on. Dave had his back to this, but for a few minutes was aware of all the sounds of confusion as tables were chosen, seats moved, umbrellas and handbags stowed and re-stowed, while above it all rose the voice of the organiser as she rounded up the laggards and tried to create some kind of order. The young girl with the wire-wool hair seemed to know exactly what was required. Amidst the shuffling and rattling and muttering, she moved quietly and efficiently, knowing it was tea and biscuits that was needed—and quickly.

Dave glanced around. Old ladies, old men, old people. No difference any more. Plastic macs wrap frail bodies; weak eyes peer round the room; faded smiles and nods; hands and heads tremble as cups are raised. Outside, the rain filtered slowly down, swirling in the narrow streets. A boy of no more than seven or eight dashed past the cafe full-tilt, head down against the wind and rain, his hair stuck down flat over his forehead, his shoes splashing on the gleaming pavement. Little idiot, thought Dave, he'll be soaked. He noticed Joan smiling at one of the old ladies and was following her gaze when he saw the old man sitting at the next window table.

He sat half-turned away from his companions at the table as though not wishing to join in their tea-time chatter. Hand on knee, head up, he gazed steadily out of the window over the promenade and beach, out into the mist and rain. His features were strong, though seamed and

13

riven like an ancient eroded hillside, and, in spite of his age, he sat erect and tall. Dave watched as a woman who sat beside him leaned forward and picked up his cup. Then she took his hand and carefully placed the cup in it. The old man slowly raised the cup to his lips and drank, then lowered the cup. His companion took the cup from his hand and replaced it in the saucer. Dave heard the cafe noises, the clink of spoon on cup, cup on saucer, the flutter of conversation, wrap themselves around him once again.

"Let's go," he said to Joan. He found that he was already standing. She stared at him, then began to collect her things.

"We're going, are we?" But Dave was already moving towards the door. She went to the counter and paid for their coffee. Dave stood, holding open the cafe door for her and, as she passed, she heard him say quietly and bitterly, as though to himself:

"Take them out, dust them down and put them back, like useless bloody ornaments."

Startled, she said, nodding back towards the old folk, "What, them?"

He shrugged and turned away. "Yes, them too." Outside, as they passed the first cafe window, he glanced up and saw through the glass the face of the old man, still blindly gazing out, out into infinity, and beside it the ghostly image of his own face. Yes, he thought with grim humour, them too.

Then the wind and rain claimed them, the relentless thump-thump of the fairground music filled the air, and arm in arm, heads down, they ran, their shoes splashing on the gleaming pavement.

14

POEMS

William-John Deerin

THE RUTHLESS SEA

In Memoriam Hart Crane
(committed suicide, April 27th, 1932)

What demons haunt your conflict?
The balance sits knife-edged.
Only a whisper can be catastrophic:
A life held flimsily? Ledged

Against its realities, perceived, bifocal.
A compass point in bleak direction:
Diffused, spinning from a vantage point.
And height; a sense of linear perfection

That drops despair to a red spot,
And ruthless as the sea.
April, your final month ticked silently.
The waves rolled, no longer an enemy.

Only then came the clarity,
An ironic sense of purpose, harmony.
You grasped the moment, the ship's stern.
And quietly taking off your coat, stepped into the sea.

THE HIDDEN LOCHAN

We discovered it quite by accident
Between two walking hills. Trapped rain
Its like before we'd never seen, yet
Too small to be regarded or even named.

It lay day lazy and crazy blue,
Stilled by its own security. How we
Searched for days like that, amid old
Landscapes and fragile obsessions.

As dusk fell we lit our considerations
And sparked ideas across our tiny
Universe. Sometimes a light surprised us
As we explored love's limitations.

We felt the night turn cold
As ideas dimmed with consequence;
The lochan, still tranquil and absolute,
Disturbed only by the occasional nightfly.

LOW-FLYING JETS

Looking down on the edge of Lochaber
I trace the flight-path of a flock of phantoms
As they tear open the air's skin and scatter
The sea-loch with a million decibels.

And faster than the fastest swift
They twist in the landscape
In a deadly pirouette. Birds of prey
More lethal than nature ever intended.

As proverbial as a will o' the wisp
With a sting in the tail, they scar the sky.
Any debris they leave behind is
Instantly obsolete and always accidental.

Each intimidates the atmosphere
Like an escaped balloon. Space invaders
Of my personal space. Marauding midges
That have cracked the speed of sound.

They flirt the mountain's ragged edge
Always a hair's breadth from disaster.
Speedfreaks on their rollercoaster.
Dambusters looking for a dam.

THE ISLAND VISIT

We sailed in early under a freezing fog
Between landscapes once patched with shadows
Of Atlantic mists—and stood again on land where no tree grows.
Our path carved its way through scurvy-grass while bog
Asphodels braved cold centuries of heather and tasselweed.
We found MacNeil behind his croft stacking rough-cut peat
Against its bleak white walls. We drank his whisky neat
And toasted absent friends beside a roaring fire and took no heed
Of the coming storm, of shark-finned waters or Atlantic breakers
As they crashed against the skerries. Our talk was of the old days,
Of women loved and lost. Of MacNiven and his crazy ways
And how once in Glasgow we lost Culrain, MacNab the
        undertaker's
Son. Catriona sang and Chrissie cried. We laughed into the night's
Dark hours. MacNeil fiddled sadly as we put the world to rights.

AT HUGH MACDIARMID'S COTTAGE

The air is clear here, cuts thin
As a scalpel and shivers naked
Through the coppiced rowans you planted
Along with a myriad of wild seed that
Grew like a parable. And the rose so white,
A *memoriam*. Inside, conjured images
Carry us across the reaches of your poetry.
We seek out the stars, still glittering, bright.

The room sits at tangents with your genius.
Here, the old poets came, beckoning new starbursts.
Rows of detective novels disguise your cunning—
You explored the universe, magnified it with your
Depth of eye. No microcosm was beyond your reach.
I sit down where Yevtushenko sat and listen,
My ear to a shell—hearing the voices,
Crystallised, and raised, like a beach.

SUMMER MADNESS

It was beneath the warplanes that first we met.
One searching for adventure, the other a home.
Our paths crossed like a swastika, but we learned
In the desert heat that love sometimes goes like that.

She resisted my advances, destroyed my strategy,
But still we loved. After a long hot summer the war stopped.
Men returned to their homes searching for their wives.
Looking back I often wonder how we won both battles.

18

MUTINOUS GHOSTS

There are no memories in your soul.
The dreams we held, not so long ago
Have turned against us,
Mutinous ghosts of summer.

You are incomplete as you stand before me.
Your nakedness is the shadow you left lost
In our city streets. The flower you wear in your hair
Is no longer the gateway to our paradise.
There is no temptation to cultivate your offering.

The day has passed when I remember
Your breasts in hunger.
My eyes were blurred with your treason.
Your nakedness is the reality of my lust.

MISTAKEN IDENTITY
(Bay of Biscay, 1972)

Once in light conversation I was asked quite coolly,
You're a German, aren't you, do you know any terrorists?

Sorry, I said, you've got the wrong country.
Though I admit to knowing Ted MacFadyen, a right holy terror.

The fedayeen! Isn't that that lot from Palestine?
Sorry, I said, you've got the wrong country.

You don't look Hebrew. Have you lived in Germany long?
Sorry, I said, you've got the wrong country.

Your English is quite good for someone with your background.
Yes, I agreed. It's the vowels. And of course the history.

19

ON JOHN SILKIN'S POETRY READING
AT THE ELPHINSTONE HOTEL, BIGGAR

Beneath black-stained timber beams
In a space once occupied by MacCaig
And Annand, a small man stands—Jew
Among Gentiles—his half-moon eyes
Prey to a pendulum of white willowy hair.
Copper lamps illuminate his venerable stare.

He builds his poems from old stones,
Lupins, butterflies, bric-a-brac and guilt.
Each one in turn an accomplice and an alibi.
I watch and listen, his words cut through my
Silence. Our doubting eyes meet accidently.
Between stanzas chairs creak irreverently.

Here is no dialogue; no union for his dead.
His voice rings the middle distance. "Man is a
Figment of God's imagination." A smile, the unmentionable
Mentioned. Even Gamaliel had the wit to test theory
With time. He did not draw on your conclusion.
He had no truck with fantasy or self-delusion.

My mind drifts to another time, another poet.
Sitting in Cordy's, under an East Anglian sun,
Reading Wain's *Wildtrack*: "Speak to me tense
Poet from your visonary gloom." Sing your song
Of snowflakes, office whores and Jahvist Jews
Linked eternally by your ecclesiastic ruse.

Now, turning back through images of Treblinka,
Three times denial rung the roost. The road from
Ur, Damascus and Jerusalem is no meeting place
For the Samaritan in you. Our paths now crossed,
We share in our time a few brief moments
As you travel through your tiny continents.

THREE TALES

Grace Sim

THE WOLF

Joan sighed. The day stretched before her, an endless desert without an oasis in sight. Her small cottage was vacuumed, scrubbed and polished until it sparkled. Monotony was the recipe of the day. She felt bored and depressed. Perhaps my granddaughter Melissa might visit, she thought. Although that won't be very uplifting. She used to be such a bright, beautiful child. She could see her now—a toddler dressed in red, blue eyes sparkling, blonde curls bouncing, always laughing. I used to call her my little Red Riding Hood.

Now, at sixteen, she resembled a black stick insect. She dieted continuously, and would wear nothing but black, as if in permanent mourning for her lost good humour. Melissa's habitual sulky expression, when she did visit, made it obvious her grandmother's house was the last place she wished to be. Her conversation was punctuated with "It's not fair" and "Why me?" She didn't have a chip on her shoulder—she had an oak tree.

Just then, Joan heard the door bell. She hurriedly opened the door and gasped in astonishment. A tall dark wolf stepped inside and closed the door. Joan looked up at him, temporarily paralysed with shock. She tried to scream but no sound would come. She backed away but he followed until she was imprisoned in his strong arms. The wolf leaned over her. She could feel his hot breath on her cheek. His face came closer and closer. She could see his strong white teeth. She shuddered as they approached her mouth. His eyes were large and hypnotic. She could see her reflection in them.

She tried to look away. She felt that she was drowning in those dark brown eyes, but she found she was unable to withdraw her gaze or close her own eyes. As Joan looked closer she found her reflection had been replaced by the reflection of herself forty years ago. Her face was unlined, her hair was long and glossy chestnut, her figure was slim and sensual. She was filled with long-forgotten emotions. These feelings flooded through her and her fears faded away . . . .

She was abruptly brought back to the present when the door bell rang. The wolf ordered, "Get rid of whoever it is." Joan gave a nervous giggle and hurried to open the door. Melissa stared in amazement. Her grandmother gabbled an excuse: "Sorry, Melissa! I have a visitor. I'm just going out. I've an important appointment and I'm running late." Then she rudely slammed the door in Melissa's face.

Melissa stood open-mouthed and gazed at the door. "She's flipped! Time she was in a nursing home," she muttered. Shrugging her shoulders she slouched back down the path, banging the gate behind her.

Later, as she scuffled her way through the leaves on the forest path, she heard the roar of a motorbike behind her. She threw herself to one side and caught a glimpse of the couple as they zoomed past. Melissa's face flickered momentarily into life. The pillion passenger was vaguely familiar. An attractive female, with long slim legs encased in black thigh-length boots. Her head was flung back, her chestnut hair streaming behind her. Melissa felt a pang of envy as she saw how this glamorous creature's curvaceous body clung like a second skin to the leather-clad rider. She thought he looked a bit of a hunk, with long black hair and piercing dark eyes. "Bet he's got a tattoo. It's not fair," Melissa grumbled. "He never even noticed me. Nothing exciting ever happens to me."

Then they were gone. All that was left was the faint sound of laughter and the rustle of leaves drifting down onto the path. Melissa sighed, the inanimate expression returning to her face. Hands deep in pockets, eyes downcast, kicking moodily at the leaves, she headed home.

THE WOODCUTTER

The woodcutter stopped. He could feel the familiar tightness in his chest again. Try to do less, his G.P. had advised. "Have you thought about retiring?" Thought about it?— he had nightmares thinking about it. His work was his whole life. Without work he was nothing. As a child his mother used to count the years until he could leave school and get a job. He could hear her now: "Just four more years and you'll be earning your keep."

It was the most important day of his life, that first day in the forest. He loved the tall trees towering above him, the soft green moss underfoot, the steady rhythm of the axe at work, the smell of the woodsmoke. Now he had the forest all to himself. No one else wanted to be a woodcutter.

Retire. He thought about it again. It was like death, it gave him the shivers even to contemplate it.

If he retired he might never see his girl again. He'd watched her since she was a child toddling. Her golden skin dappled by the sun's reflections through the leaves. How he had looked forward to seeing her skipping through the trees. The years had passed so quickly. Now she was a beautiful woman. He'd been in love with her for years, but what would she see in him but a stupid old man who could do nothing with his life but cut down trees?

He would also miss the conversations with her grandmother who lived in a cottage right in the middle of the woods. He always called in for a cup of coffee and some home-baked scones when he was over that way. He repaid her by taking her a sack of logs every visit. She was a modern grandmother, very spritely for her age. She was doing an Open University course at the moment. She seemed to enjoy talking to him. At one time he felt she would have liked the relationship to have developed a bit further, but how could it develop when he'd fallen in love with her granddaughter?

And then, if he retired, the forest would be empty. No one would be watching for the wolf who lurked behind the trees. Following her. The wolf always made himself scarce when he appeared with his axe over his shoulder. He could not leave her to the wolf. If he couldn't keep her safe, he would rather she was dead.

He must keep her safe. He could feel the pain beginning again. Spreading across his chest like tendrils of ivy, constricting his throat, making it difficult to breathe. He ignored the pain and began to sharpen his axe. The steady sound of the whetstone on the metal soothed him. But he would have to hurry. The pain was getting worse but he didn't have time to rest. His love would be along any moment now.

PENGALLON WOODS

It was a brave individual who entered Pengallon Woods at night. There was a dark sinister atmosphere about them. In the inns and market-places, tales were told of people who had entered them and never been seen again. But then, the Cornish folk are very superstitious, and renowned for spinning yarns.

One cold winter day, Emily Ward, a kitchen maid at Porthmellion Farm, set out on her journey home to Pengallon. Under her arm she carried a bundle of her mistress's old clothes, for her mother. Although she left at three o' clock the daylight was almost gone. The sky, an angry brooding purple, heralded an approaching storm. Emily drew her shawl more tightly about her as the first flakes of snow flirted with the wind. As she skirted Pengallon Woods she shivered with apprehension. The branches seemed like menacing arms reaching out to drag her into a deadly embrace. There was a lull and then the storm struck. The snow twisted and twirled about her, while the now gale-force wind endeavoured to blow her over. Emily fell, stumbled to her feet and fell again. She was desperately tired, her shawl heavy with encrusted snow. It would be so easy to allow her eyes to close, lie down and fall asleep. She knew she must find shelter.

Overcoming her inbred fear of Pengallon Woods she pushed her way through the ferns, brambles and dense undergrowth and found herself on a narrow track. Emily shook the snow from her shawl and felt her fears lessening. Relieved to be sheltered from the storm, she decided the frightening tales were all fantasies. All that she had to do was stay near the edge of the woods, another mile and she would be home. She was a little warmer now, and smiled as she thought how she would brag about being unafraid of Pengallon Woods.

It was then that Emily heard the noise. She stopped for a moment and listened. All was quiet. Then quite distinctly she heard it again. Crack! As if someone had stood on a brittle branch. Emily hurried on. The noises followed her. She started to run and within seconds had lost the track and her bearings. She stumbled on, branches catching and tearing her clothes, all the time aware that somebody or something was close behind her and getting closer. As she glanced over her shoulder her foot caught on the root of a tree and she fell, wrenching her ankle and striking her head on the ground. Dazed, she lay still. Her breathing was ragged with terror and panic. Then she heard a low growling noise and looked up to see, standing over her, a huge black wolf-like animal. It stood above her, hair upright on the back of its neck, nose curled back from bared teeth now just inches from her face. Emily could already feel those sharp incisors tearing into her flesh. Please God let it be quick! She closed her eyes, an involuntary sob coming from deep in her throat, before she passed out.

The animal's growl slowly faded, it lowered its head and sniffed at the girl's hands covering her face. Then it began to lick her fingers. Emily recovered consciousness as strong arms lifted her. Head throbbing, ankle aching, she turned her face into her rescuer's shoulder and clasped her arms around his neck.

Emily pulled her shawl around her and hurried up the path to her mother's cottage. It was still bitterly cold but the snow had stopped. She lifted the latch. The smell of baking filled her nostrils. She realised she was ravenous. Her mother's back was towards her.

"Hello, mother, sorry I'm late."

Her mother swung round, eyes staring, the colour draining from her face.

"Emily, child, is it really you? Where have you been?" Her voice broke into sobs.

"I was caught in the storm, mother, and sheltered in Pengallon Woods. There's nothing to be upset about. Here I am safe, and only a little late."

Her mother wiped her eyes. "Come, lass, over to the fire, sit down, take off your shawl. We need to talk. You're not a little late. You're a year late."

Emily sat down, speechless, and loosened her shawl. There was a faint sound. They both gazed in astonishment. There, nestling in her arm, was a baby, a beautiful baby, with dark eyes and a mass of black hair.

Ian Hunter

NOT LIKE THAT

Because you can't bear to look
at those photographs
Edged black and white slices
of a life
Bound by frames
Showing her smile,
like the sun cracking open
Her face,
like a bulb, burning bright
Her hair,
wild, plugged-in
Her glow
Her life
Her life

Because you can't bear to look
at her now
Hair grown back,
clinging and lifeless
Still vomiting
Body bloated by drugs
Balloon face almost bursting
as if swelled by the energy
that belonged in her body
This human slow-puncture
Has resisted the medical patch
Still leaking
Still leaking

Because you can't bear to put
her into the ground like that
The only hope left,
is she dies like she lived,
even a little bit
Glowing
So take her away
and leave the bottles and syringes
behind
with her father
and wait for the end to come

SUCCESSFUL WOMAN EXECUTIVE TYPE

Since my wife
buys the cream
uses the hair spray
and the sanitary towels
aerodynamically designed
with special wings

She's entitled
when she triumphs
to turn to the camera
clench her fists
say "Yes!"
then glide all
the way home

HAPPY BABY

Your

smile

is

too

heavy

for

your

head

to

hold

so

      it

wobbles

      from

side

      to

side

THE PEOPLE NOT THE GARDEN

In the city where you live
your house eats half your benefits
as Power Cards
in the constant fight
against the black fungus
on the walls

In the house where you live
you sleep through the night
in an armchair
pulled into the centre of
the room
far from the damp walls
and your wet bed upstairs

In the city where you live
you can always visit
the museum with the Zen Garden
where men flew over from Japan
to rake the stones
in a special way

SEARCH AND RESCUE

Robert Hume

The fence came first. Its wires whipped the windscreen, gouging stars where the rusty barbs struck. Then the horizon did its somersaults—fast, then with soaring pauses, then with two juddering swings, the last ending with the falling squeal of the suspension. When he was aware—his first awareness—of seeing the world as he remembered it through the windscreen, he could see where they had come. The fence up there, pulled part-way down the embankment: one cable looping up ridiculously towards the sky, the others pulled together by the car's breakthrough, with the old wooden posts dragged out and down at either side; and a twin-track flattened through the coarse grey-green grass halfway towards where they lay. And, from the wheel arch, the sliver of live wood wrenched from the heart of the dead as it snapped, a broken post stood to attention just at the edge of his vision. All this in a second. Then.

They. The children?

Fast as the safety webbing would allow, he turned around. Another picture, but more familiar. And more explanation. The sound. The sound had been Quilly, sobbing. "What happened? What happened? What . . . why . . . ?" But all very quietly, like some shared secret. No damage there. The harness had done its work.

Patti was different. "Patti! Are you O.K.?" He strained to speak the words clearly, separately, not to sound frightened. As he stretched round the headrest to see, he became dimly aware of the dull pain across his shoulders. But Patti. As he leaned over, Patti was looking past him, into a middle distance. The glasses were at an angle less than askew. But the harness, as he looked at its central operation patch, had been on, had been functioning. Was it just that he had become lost in the moment, adrift in events? It had happened so many times before—autobooks, games, vu-thrus—sunk in them with no manual override, why sometimes he'd simply had to shake him to get his attention.

"PATTI!" His Sunday, why-do-I-have-to-raise-my-voice tone.

"Yes . . . ." From far away. "How did that happen?"

The question was matter of fact, but it brought him back to the situation. As it sunk in it also seemed to quieten Quilly's sob to a whimper.

"I don't know." But even in speaking it became the lie. The wrong road, the wrong conditions, the wrong speed . . . too many wrongs.

"But John . . . "

"Yes, it's all right. Look." He'd have to work fast now. Patti's brow, furrowed, questions ready to tumble; and they'd set Quilly off, nothing surer. "Look at the readout. There." There on the dash display, its colour and brightness level specially chosen to be reassuring, was the car's message to them.

BEACON ACTIVE. RESCUE ALERTED.

Quilly was silent. Her eyes flickered from one side of the message to the other, the winking asterisks its key component for her. Patti too had paused, thinking. Best not to bother what. Time to reinforce the message, continue reassuring them.

"You know what that means, don't you?" Best not wait for a reply. "It means that someone will be coming for us.

33

Soon. Very soon. That's the great thing about this car—it's a smart car, it can think for itself. It's already sent out a message, let the Carries know that we're in trouble, that we need help. They'll come and fix us, help us get home. You want that, don't you?"

Too fast, too fast, he thought, and a bit too desperate at the end. Would it work? Quilly's eyes had widened—O.K. there. Patti nervously cleared his throat.

"But if it's so smart why did we crash? And why can't we just drive back up onto the road?" Thankfully he didn't look aggressive so much as puzzled.

"Well, you can see the answer to your second question there, can't you? Look at the display. See the big warning box, DO NOT DRIVE. The car wouldn't let us drive now even if we wanted to. It's probably that post wedged in beside the wheel, it's either wrecked the wheel or the control electronics."

Reference to the post brought Quilly back to life. "Let's move it!" Her hand reached towards the harness patch.

"NO. We can't leave the car. We have to stay inside it." As Quilly's lip trembled, his voice softened. "Inside the car is our safe place. The car will look after us. It's programmed to keep us safe." Her face relaxed slowly, hearing the right words.

"So why did we crash?" Patti returned to his analysis.

"We weren't on an A-road. If we'd been on one of those, the car would have taken us home just about by itself. But there'd been a bulletin, things were busy, so I took us on a short cut, one of the old roads. And before you ask, you were in such a hurry to catch something on the screen, and Quilly was tired, so I decided to go this way." Patti subsided in the seat, grudging any anticipation of his interrogative method. Well, that would help. Still, guilt was

34

a many-faceted thing. "Anyway, the car's smart enough to work out our position by triangulation." (The t-word would get Patti's mathematical juices working.) "It may take a little longer, but they'll still be here for us. And soon. Here, why don't you look up the response details in the manual." He rummaged in amongst the documentation glossies. The salesman had joked about those, but right now they were just what was needed. He pulled out the slim, bright booklet headed *Search and Rescue*. He could see Patti's eyes widen as he caught sight of the Carrie logo, then fix themselves on the holopix cover. With any luck, that would keep him busy for a while. He hadn't realised it, but nipping his questions in the bud like that had taken Quilly's interest out of consideration too: her eyes were blinking their way towards sleep. So, now he was to be left with his own thoughts.

They weren't hard to define. They began to shape themselves as a series of questions Φal would ask. He'd heard her first one, he swore, when he took the turn-off ("The A-roads are there to make our lives safer. Why stop them from doing that?"). But it had been such a good, spur-of-the-moment idea. The freedom, not hearing the click as each terminal went past, feeling the steering-wheel turn to his command only, the power of the engine beneath his foot. But then, like the quiet insistence of her voice as they argued, he had felt it slowly turn against him. First had been the countryside itself—the grass more brown than green, the hills sharper, craggier than they first seemed, the strange mixture of dull colours. Then the road. First its width had started to vary, then its colour—patches here and there, half-started repairs working themselves into holes, puddles of unspecified depth. And occasionally water running across, streaming through gouts of mud and god-knows-what-else; sometimes flattened by some random action into incipient ruts. But worst of all seemed the atmosphere—as though the place was waiting for something bad to happen to you.

That hadn't just been him, his nervy imagination. The children had noticed it too, with those crows. Metallic grey they seemed to be, fighting over the scraps of something run into the road. He'd seen them first, one pulling at what looked like a piece of pink elastic, which stretched but would not release its hold on the road. The others scuttling round it, waiting to grab purchase, but canny to get their work done for them first. The car's progress had set them flying off, but only at the last possible minute. And even as they wheeled away, it seemed as though they were looking at them: quizzically, analytically, perhaps waiting for the chance to show hostility. Patti and Quilly had laughed, but nervously. He'd joined in—after all, it was his adventure— but the pause they'd all felt afterwards had said clearly that they were out of their own territory.

Suddenly something at the edge of his vision. He jerked to catch it. Was it that crow? No, it looked to be made of stone. No, it was the glow from the message which had increased. Looking round himself, he realised that an afternoon twilight was gathering around them. Shadows were forming: what colour there had been had lost even the vestiges of brightness. And, with surprise, he realised that the car was lighting itself up, compensating for this outer darkness, becoming another, older kind of beacon in itself. His heart was so full with the knowledge of this that he yearned to tell Patti and Quilly about it, but checked himself. No sense in arousing them with a positive image which might slowly be snuffed out.

Anyway, soon that glow would make it harder to make

anything out in the growing twilight. Maybe his eyes would start playing tricks on him. He looked again for the crow, like some kind of landmark. There it was—did it seem closer, or was it just the light? Its eye seemed sharper too, beadily locked on his. No, his imagination surely.

Then, right across from it. Lights. Headlights. For them, or just local traffic? He reached out to signal, somehow, but even as he did so remembered. He couldn't. The car would stop him. It had sent its signal, and now awaited its own rescuers. A wave of anger and bitter frustration ran through him. He would have to watch as the car went past. He would have to explain it . . . ! How could . . . ?

"Yeeeeees! It's the Carries!" Patti's shout broke through his anger, and followed the sweep of their lights as it curved down into the valley, up over the embankment and to where they lay. Squinting past the lights, he could see the illuminated logo. At once he became aware of Quilly's giggling. Now both of them were talking together at once, just out of sheer relief. His attention, as his head cleared, fixed itself on what he could now see was an all-terrain WD. Both its doors opened together, but it was no faceless heroes who appeared. Just two large men in glossy corporate overalls. They did have the calf-boots from the ad though, he noticed as they came over to them. Both also wore broad grins.

"You've had some trouble, but we're here now." The older one was the first to speak, as the driver window slowly let itself down. "That's the motto, isn't it, rely on us for your rescue." His younger assistant's delivery was less polished. However, like some mechanical sesame the passenger door creaked open, the harness patches sprang apart, and the children were beside him in a second. He took their hands, seemingly unconscious of their infatu-

37

ated stares. "It's the rescue module for you, Quilly and Patti. Do you want to see how it works?" They seemed almost to trot their way, hands in his hands, to the WD, and could be dimly seen through what looked like a perspex bubble towards the rear.

"Now, John, you know what the drill is, don't you?" The older one was by his ear now, reaching in to press the code for bonnet release. There was a hiss of air, then he returned with what looked for all the world like a suitcase turned inside out. "This is the Manager unit. It comes with us. You have to stay here to guard the body shell."

"But Φal . . . "

"She'd want you to do it."

"Patti? Quilly?"

"They're safe, safe with us."

His face relaxed, hearing the right words. It was still upturned as the Carrie walked away. Still upturned when the children waved through the perspex as the WD began to climb the embankment. They could see the glow rimmed by his jaw. As he looked at the tail-lights heading off, he became aware how the glow had dimmed, of his dying beacon. Outside he could just make out the jerky, wheeling movements as the crow was joined by another, darker one.

THE MANGO

Murray Davidson

for Paula's special birthday

The Mango.
Magnificent, succulent,
sweet and delicious—
perfect fruit of sunshine.
Of every fruit
on every branch
we watched the bitter green
transform to brilliant sunshine.
A ferment of ripening sunlight
and rain,
a chalice of laughter and tears.
A dial to which all heads turned,
impatiently chasing time.

The old tree we knew with intimate dedication.
The position and precision
of each ripening fruit
was quietly noted,
or noisily discussed
in a fervour of excitement,
as every village eye
wished and willed
the most enormous pregnant fruit to fall
when only they were witness,
only they were blessed
a glimpse of nature's dance
through the perfect light of day.

The rains soaked through
a dusty, pensive earth
to nourish seeds and roots
which thirsty sucked
to feed the sap
which rose and spread
through life and limb
and branch and twig
to each and every leaf
which stretched
with open glance
for sunshine,
warmth
and rain.

The rains brought Africa to life.
Insects nurtured
through dry winters days
sprang nourished
by the warm summer rain.
A sudden explosion of life
on a half expectant world.
Great black wasps,
machines of sting.
Heavy flying giant beetles,
noisy and incongruous
like limping injured Sopworths.
Mosquitos and flies
and flies and more flies.
Flies that bit and chased and nipped
and flies that laid their eggs
which hatched
'neath unsuspecting skin.
Enormous flies that out of nowhere sprang,
blind to all but one sweet scent
and one intent,
to search and seek that newly ripened mango.

No one with any sense
ate mangos in the daytime.
No one,
unless they locked their doors
and plugged the holes
in window nets,
and sat content
to peel the skin
with blade and thumb
and slice the flesh
let loose sweet juice
and watch unfold
the clouds of angry flies,
incessantly, vainly,
tortuously trying to defy
each perfect window net.

The old mango tree
stood amid our cliff-top garden,
a proud view from our tumbledown,
faded colonial home.
A careful connoisseur of heaven's fruit
had one day brought
a precious seed
from land afar,
to plant and rest
to grow and care
as searching roots
would anchor strong
from wind and rain
most noble mango tree.
Whilst seasons change
and this old house
reverts to sand and stone,
so year on year
our mango tree
bears fruit a little more.

We watch each fruit
with guarded breath
each day and moonlit night,
(for time can still recall of years
when darkness waned
and morning cried,
"A Thief!",
a thief has stripped the mango bare
and made off with them all!)
and then,
as if by sight and scent,
or primal intuition,
in perfect time with nature's task
we charge forthwith and plunder.
Scrambling, clambering,
picking, dropping,
eating, laughing,
singing, joking,
filling baskets,
sweetest mango,
panting, sweating,
blazing sunshine,
pluck and pick
and pick and pluck
till spoils and all
of this sweet tree
fills five and twenty baskets.

All too soon the tree stands light,
bereft of last year's purpose.
A mango growing
sunshine ripens
rains a falling
boughs a weaken
fruit comes crashing
seeds of fortune
seek the earth,

prostrate in hope,
take root.

As evening falls
the tree stands robbed, silhouetted,
bathed in midsummer moonlight.
We sit replete in silence satisfied
too full to move
while crickets shrill to Africa's
intense chaotic rhythm.
As the thundering ocean
sends wave upon wave
crashing on the rocks below,
the darkness issues
countless wordless whispers
as mosquitos
gently dance upon
the faintest evening breeze.
With stealth they seek
the warmest blood
which pulses 'neath
our fragile skin
to plunder pierce
each gasping vein
they chance descend,
in silence gain
their frenzied feast intoxicant—
erythrocytic gorge.

Stars cascade
through an ink-black sky
on a world ablaze with moonlight.
We listless sigh
and past reflect
the seasons' change
which brought to life
through scorching rain
this annual celebration.

The season of rain,
The season of change,
The season of storms and thunder.
Warm winds blow
and the fruit trees grow,
in the season of the glorious Mango.

POEMS

Eileen Whitelaw

OFF-KEY

Hills, clouds and wind
    flow and float;
Swallows scythe the high air;
The warm blue summer falls like silk.
Only the oyster-catcher
    searches the space.

HAIKU

In the dusty book
A pressed and perfect petal.
    Its fragrance quite gone.

A crumpled cushion,
Still warm, it contains your shape.
    Why the cool disdain?

WATCHING THE LOCH IN WINTER

Hard brittle notes encase the geese.
Dead leafs skid on sharp ice.
Shafting grasses spike the sheeted margin
Where blackened sedge
    holds summer's nests.
Ducks waddle and skiddle,
    flirt and fight,
Then break for the bank;
And across Coulter, cold clouds stream.

7 A.M.

The earth lies quiescent
In the blue darkness that heralds dawn.
A soft damp wind billows through the
                    cloisters
Only to die on the distant wall.
A bird calls once before its time, and
  the bell's echoes throng the air.
Within the scene is set in light and
                    warmth and colour;
Faint fragrance of flowers and candlewax
And timeless compulsive words flow up
                    and beyond dim arches.
Yet still the ceaseless struggle.
Our outer tranquillity,
So akin to complacency,
Is but a facade.
To rid ourselves of ourselves,

Attain the unattainable,
Enthrone humility in our proud hearts
Where thoughts of God jostle
                    with thoughts of hell
And our prayers waste on the arid
                    desert air
Of self-concern . . . .
This we hide from others.
But yet we know
Of one, more willing to hear than we
                    are to pray—
And herein is the still centre of
                    our being;
Without which, indeed, we live in vain.

THE BRIDGE

Agnes Thomson

It was growing dark, but not quite dark enough. A few lights were beginning to come on in houses in the distance, houses filled with normal people carrying on with their normal lives. There were still a few hardy people walking from one end of the bridge to the other, in spite of the cold and the wind gusting around them. Peter looked at the grey water far below him, and wished that they would all go home.

The old man with the dog stopped a few feet away from him.

Just what I need, thought Peter. Some old sod looking for somebody to talk to.

But the old man ignored him and stared out over the water, his white hair flicking across his weatherbeaten face. The dog settled at his master's feet, laid his head on his front paws and closed his eyes.

Peter resigned himself to a long wait and sighed deeply.

"Cheer up! It might never happen."

"You'll be telling me next that every cloud has a bloody silver lining!"

The old man looked hurt.

"I'm sorry," said Peter. "I didn't mean to . . . ."

"Forget it son, we all have our off days." He looked away, towards the north shore.

Peter felt the need to make up for his rudeness.

"Nice wee dog."

"Aye, he is that, but he's getting a bit old now. I don't

know what I'll do when he goes."

"Can't you get another one?"

"It wouldn't be fair to a dog. I might not last out his lifetime and I wouldn't like to do that—you know, leave him wondering. Still, I suppose I'll see Laddie out."

"You look as if you've got a few good years left in you."

"What age do you think I am?"

Peter hated being asked that question.

"Sixty-three? Sixty-four?"

"I'll be seventy-five on my birthday!"

Peter was grimly amused by the old man's obvious pride.

"You've got a good thirty years on me."

"Forty-five? Man, you're just a pup! Mind you, it can be a queer age to be."

"It's a bloody stupid age!"

"Aye, maybe, but it passes."

Peter turned back to stare at the water.

"Sometimes it's too late."

The old man fumbled in his coat pocket. Laddie lifted his head and pricked up his ears hopefully, but it was a pack of cigarettes, not mints, that he drew out. Peter automatically started to refuse the proffered pack—he'd stopped four years ago—when the irony of the situation struck him. He almost, but not quite, laughed out loud.

He felt lightheaded and unreal as the nicotine buzzed straight to his brain. He wanted the old man to go now and leave him alone to savour the cigarette.

"Won't your wife be wondering where you are?"

"Oh, I lost my wife five years ago. That's why Laddie is so important to me. He's my best pal now. What about you —are you married?"

Peter nodded.

"Does she know where you are?"

"No."

"Won't she be worrying about you?"

"She's done a lot of that lately."

"Is she a good woman, then, your wife?"

"Too bloody good for me!"

"Well, I suppose she's the only one who has the right to decide that."

Peter grunted but made no comment. He noticed that the old man was trying hard to control the shivering that had taken hold of his body.

"You're freezing, man. You should be at home with a hot drink, putting your feet up."

"Oh, I'm in no hurry. I think I'll hang on here for a wee while."

Peter laughed. He knew when he was beaten. "You're a stubborn old bugger."

"Aye, I've been called that—and worse."

"C'mon, old timer, I'll treat you to a brandy."

"Now you're talking! North or South?"

POEMS

Marilyn Scanlan

THE MECHANIC

"Jenny, how did our children
Survive, when you feed me so
Roughly?"
She could not answer.
She had fed so many.
Twenty years of spoon-feeding.
An expectant mother again
And spoon-feeding the last.
A life caught up in keeping
Others alive, even with death
So near.

OCEANS APART

Most times you go off
In your blue motorboat.
Speeding here and there.
I don't know where.
You always come back.
Come back to me. The
Woman in the yellow
Bathing-cap. Easily seen,
Stuck out like a buoy,
Your marker.

At first it didn't matter.
I never looked for your
Return.

SAD FACES

This is the tale of a despairing woman,
A victim of seemingly motiveless crimes.

Her wardrobe is full of unsuitable fashion,
Her mind full of hints from old magazines.

She's studied the books about putting on make-up,
Expertly hiding all perceived flaws.

She's looking for singles in her own age group;
A long-lasting love, who'll return after dawn.

When she was younger, she felt so excited:
Butterflies rose like bubbling champagne.

Time grows inside her: a dark heavy wasteland,
With each sterile meeting, with each raw exchange.

DANGER ZONE

We all turned to look, some
Tip-toed to gain a clearer view.
Janice's buttocks were pressed
To the panes, as the greenhouse
Shook with rhythmic force.

Molly, worried about broken glass,
Cataloguing the injuries that
Could occur, watched nervously;
One eye on the phone, ready to call
An ambulance if the worst did happen.

The men in the group spoke to each
Other in low conspiratorial tones. Every
Few seconds a muffled laugh was heard.
Wives shushed and told them to behave.
No one moved or looked away.

When the greenhouse timbers gradually
Stilled, Janice and George, clothes
Straight again, neatly walked hand in
Hand, through the garden and down
To the river. Nobody said a word.

PERFECT ISOLATION

She sits in the bank,
Her thin frame hunched over the table.
Spread out before her,
The bills she cannot pay.

Her lank, straight hair
Covers her face. A young woman,
Already grey.
Heavy rings on her wedding finger.

She shakes her head.

The note-pad beside her
Is filled with sums.
She follows the columns up and down.

She shakes her head again.

A LETTER TO M

I never did tell you about
My time of complete rage.

That evening I arrived home quite late.
It was a hot night,
The light still bright at ten.
When I opened the door I knew.
I knew exactly what had happened.

You had invited friends round.
Was it a celebration?

Remember how hot it was that night?
No, maybe you don't.
All I wanted was a quick shower,
A quiet evening. You insisted that
I join the others in the garden.

That was when I saw my apple trees.
That was the moment I left you.

How could you cut so ruthlessly?
Did you not enjoy their cool shade?
I'm sure you once said you did.
Did you not enjoy the late April blossom?
Did they mean nothing to you?
Or had we never discussed it?

It was then that I didn't want you any more.
It was then that I began to despise you.

You were so pleased. A job well done.
You had asked me often to prune them.
I loved their long arms
As much as I loved yours.
But you couldn't wait.

Next morning you were still asleep.
Hungover in our apple-blossom bed.
Spoilt.

I opened the french windows and looked at the mess.
The sun beat down strongly on discarded wine glasses,
Beer cans and uneaten food.

As you slept,
I looked at my trees, which cast no doubt now.
I knew.

REACTIONS

Ethyl Smith

Kneeling beside her client's easy chair the young chiropodist smiled encouragingly at the tired face. "Right then, Mrs Brennan. If you roll down your stocking a bit, I'll ease it off for you."

Kate leaned forward, but it was a real effort, and she was glad to flop back while the stocking was removed. "Thanks, dear. I'm not so good at the bending these days. Makes me out of breath, you see."

"Just relax then. Let me do the rest." Carefully the girl placed Kate's blue-veined foot in the middle of a clean towel spread in readiness across a low footstool, and opened her black treatment bag. "You're my first appointment today, you know."

"My, I'm honoured, but what about Mrs Carmichael next door? She always likes to be first."

"Oh, I rang and rang the bell, but she seems to be out. Maybe I'll catch her after my other calls, otherwise she'll have to wait till next time."

"You're a busy girl."

"Busy? Half the time I seem to be running to stand still."

"Best way, dear. Now, when I was your age . . . ."

The girl laughed. "Yes, I've heard some of your stories. Never a dull moment, eh?"

"Well, I certainly didn't have much time to think one way or the other." Kate smiled fondly at a serious young face staring out from a fancy photo frame on the sideboard.

"And all because of him, Flying Officer Frederick Patrick Brennan. My Fred. Looks good in uniform, doesn't he?"

The girl nodded, and said, as she always did, "Fine looking man."

"Aye, and he swept me off my feet too. Bride the one year, mother the next, then a widow by the third, and do you know what, the war wasn't even over."

"I'm sorry. It must have been terrible."

"Only some of it, dear. Mind you, after fifty years the bad bits don't matter so much, not when I've so many fond memories to keep me going. But you'll understand how important these are when you're as old as me."

If I ever get there, the girl thought, as she dabbed Kate's twisted toes with surgical spirit.

Kate frowned as she watched the girl's deft fingers. Just look at mine. All bent and twisted. Arthritis has a lot to answer for. Mind you, they weren't always like this. There was a time, not that long ago, if the truth be told . . . and she allowed the picture of a fair-haired girl to grow in her mind.

"My, look at your nails."

"What was that, dear?" Reluctantly Kate drifted back to the present, and the girl giggled kindly at her puzzled look.

"Here's me talking away and thinking you're listening, and all the time you're busy dreaming. I was on about your toenails, how fast they grow. Just as well I come regularly and keep them trim, eh?"

"It's nice to see you too, dear." Kate smiled down at the crown of fair curls. Yes, she thought, and nice to hear a young voice. Pity she talks so fast though, makes her hard to follow. Come to think of it half the nonsense folk talk these days isn't worth bothering about. But she's different. She makes me laugh. Maybe I'm not in the mood today.

Maybe I should say. I wouldn't like her to think I was rude. Nice hair too, soft blonde like mine was, except mine was long and straight and tied back with a silk ribbon. Fred was forever buying me fancy ribbons. Said it made me look like a lady.

Suddenly Kate blinked as the curls on top of the girl's head seemed to wave about, almost as if they were dancing. That's odd. She blinked again. Och, don't be stupid.

But when she did look away the pink roses on the wallpaper opposite seemed to be on the move too, and Fred's photo on the sideboard, the one she looked at a hundred times a day, Fred's smiling face was almost escaping from its fancy frame.

Her mood changed. Now she seemed to be swaying ever so gently, or was it the chair? She gripped the arm rest, then dug her nails into the soft material to try and steel herself against the movement, backwards and forwards, almost like being on a swing.

She felt dizzy, and everything in the room began to swim and merge.

Opening her mouth Kate tried to speak, to tell the girl, but no sound escaped. She tried again. It was no use, and she was left in a spiralling haze of fear while the young chiropodist continued chatting and clipping until Kate's foot gave a sudden jerk.

"Steady, Mrs Brennan, I'm not hurting you, am I?" The girl looked up, then yelled, "Oh my God!" and grabbed at the slumping body in the chair.

Kate's home help rushed through from the kitchen and one glance had the stout little woman trying to help the struggling girl. "Here. Catch her head. No, not that way. Hold her steady, before she slides down any further. Now, I'll try and keep her upright. You run and phone an ambulance."

"Ambulance?"

"Yes. There's a phone in the hall. Go on. Are you stupid or something?"

The girl jumped up and ran into the hall.

"Easy, Mrs Brennan, easy. It's okay." The home help said this more for her own benefit. What's the girl doing? Can't take that long to phone.

Worse than useless, so she is . . . . "Oh, there you are. I was beginning to think you were lost. Did you get through? Is somebody coming?"

The girl nodded.

"How long will they be? Did you remember the right street and number? We don't want them going to the wrong house."

Kate heard the sharp questions and mumbled replies but they came like echoes creeping to the back of a long tunnel and held no interest, not now with this protective greyness wrapped round her like a cocoon, as comforting as any blanket, and her earlier fear all gone.

What did it matter anyway? Not when she felt tired, too tired to be bothered with this vague interruption of reality by her side. Heavy with longing for sleep, she relaxed. That was better. No reason to hold back, much more appealing to drift on, allow this greyness to cover her over and quietly disappear.

As the girl and the home help stared at Kate's white face the girl whispered, "Is she . . . ?"

The home help stiffened, the shook her head. "Don't even think it." But her fingers sought Kate's wrist just in case and her eyes swung away from the girl's open stare. There was nothing else to say, which made it seem a long time before the ambulance klaxon filled the street.

59

The journey to hospital meant nothing to Kate. She didn't even surface during her admission, and the young registrar had to content himself with an over-anxious home help who'd insisted on accompanying her unconscious client.

"Couldn't let her come by herself. Her family don't live here, you see. Not that I want you to think I'm interfering, but she relies on me, so she does. I'm her home help. Nice lady she is too, but I may as well warn you, when she wakes up it won't make much difference." She tapped her head. "Bit confused, if you get my meaning."

Not the only one, the young man thought uncharitably as he tried to fill out the admission form. This is all I need at the end of a thirty-six hour shift.

When Kate opened her eyes she was surprised to see a woman's smiling face bending over her. She was even more surprised to hear this stranger say, "Don't worry, dear. You'll be fine. Here's the doctor to see you."

A second head appeared and smiled down. "Ah, Mrs Brennan. Feeling better now?"

A man's face. A man's voice. A strange man. A young man. Kate stared at the doctor and nurse and opened her mouth to speak but nothing happened. Even when she tried to shape her tongue it just seemed to roll about inside her mouth. What was it she wanted to say anyway? It's there so it is. Come out, come out, wherever you are. She searched her memory. Something's happened, that's what it is. Then gradually she began to realise—and it's me it's happened to.

Her eyes swept back and forward across the two faces. And who are you, why are you smiling like that? I've never seen you before.

The two faces above were speaking quietly to each other,

discussing her and her only a few inches below them. Every now and again the young man would mention her name, then the woman would nod, then they'd glance at her again, then they'd both nod, almost as if they were playing some game.

I'm here, so why can't you just tell me? Do you think I'm too stupid then? If only this tongue of mine would behave itself.

Finally she gave up and looked towards the bottom of the bed. Maybe there was a clue there. This is a bed. I'm in a bed. Her agitated fingers picked at the starched white cover. And I'm lying down, and my head's on a big pillow, feels nice too, nice and soft, but I don't have a pillow like this, and this isn't my bed, so how did I get here? Somebody must have put me here. Was it these two up there?

Suddenly she remembered her big easy chair. Her eyes flicked about anxiously. And where's the sideboard gone, and where's my Fred's photo?

She felt lost, and then an idea made her glare at the two faces. Have you got my photo? Is that what you're grinning about? Think you're smart holding on to my Fred, eh? Smirking and whispering there as if I don't know what you're up to. Bending there so close that I can see right up your nose, and up your nose is not all I see. You should think black burning shame, so you should, behaving there as if I haven't the sense to understand what you're on about. I'm still able to work things out, you know. I can still think, even if you don't think I can, and if you could just hear me I'd soon wipe that stupid grin off both your faces!

But her tongue behaved as if it had a life of its own and she was forced to stare up silently as the faces seemed to grow like two great moons. She stared and stared till her focus blurred and allowed her to turn away; but that didn't help, for all she saw was the outline of another bed. Beyond that another bed and another. Nothing made any sense.

Oh God, I'm scared. What can I do? Her head was bursting from the effort of thinking. Close my eyes. That's it. Shut it all out. And she obeyed this last piece of inspiration.

The strange scene vanished. She felt better. Then out of the shadows a familiar face began to swirl and grow and sharpen till she could almost swear her Fred was as clear as if he was standing beside her. It was even tempting to open her eyes again, but that might make him disappear, so she kept the lids firmly closed. And them faces'll never guess you're hiding inside my head. They'll think you're still in that photo they stole. And a hint of cunning flitted across her brow. Our secret, eh. Just you and me.

"She's asleep now," the nurse whispered.

"Wish I was," the doctor grunted. "Not much to be gained here anyway." He stepped to the end of the bed. "No, not much to be gained here." Then, aware of the nurse's steady gaze, he began to scribble his notes.

"Anything else, doctor?" Her words were sharp as glass.

He stopped writing and looked up, even smiled politely. "No, indeed. Not for the moment. Thank you, nurse."

"Excuse me, then." She seemed about to say something else, but he'd recognised the sign and was ready with another smile, a warm smile, a please forgive me smile.

The nurse's expression softened. After all the poor man had been on call for a long time, must be tired, too tired to think straight.

She made to return his smile, then hesitated, and a still moment hung between them before she repeated, "Excuse me, then," and this time her tone was almost pitying before she bustled away to another bed.

Douglas Robertson

SEALESS SICKNESS

"If you climb to the top of that hill,
you'll be able to see it from there."

But no, nothing,
Just the usual rolling
Scenic moorland landscape.

"If you head straight out in that direction,
you'll get to Denmark," Wullie said.

And I used to believe him,
Out towards that distant tension line
Between sea and sky.

"The sky's too close to your head here,
and the clouds scrape noisily over the hills."

Offshore wheeling birds and more than
Enough headroom,
Is just what this landlocked soul requires.

I take down the box,
And in it I escape,
Creel needle,
Heart urchin,
Green stone,
Partan shell;

"Tomorrow I'll look for a higher hill."

MOUTH MUSIC

You start to sing, your voice resounds
Around the wooden room, rings in the air.

And as you sing, it recalls the time your fathers
Gathered to put voice to their music, bringing
To life their past.

Some more you sing, the words of the music
Mimic the songs of the pipes, praising the beauty
Of your land.

We dance as you sing, quick stepping and reeling
Feeling the touch of the pipers hands, hearing
The cry of the wind and the sea.

And still faster you sing, our minds dance and fly
High over kyle and sgurr, wings to carry our senses.

We listen to your song, a poignant nation's legacy
Vanity to the unbelieving ear, long may your people's
Story remain strong in your voice.

THE NEWBURGH GHOST

1.
Dry
    Seized
    Rusted
        Iron

Red
    Petrified
    Pulseless
        Heart

2.
Revolution gave life to the mill,
Water now makes it still,

The wheel turns full circle,

Water gave life to the mill,
Revolution now makes it still,

The wheel turns full circle.

3.
The worn leather gloves are placed
Upon the long wooden bench, set to
Handle another hard day's work.

A row of grain shovels stand at
The ready, an army at attention
For the morning's inspection.

Everything is protected and preserved
By a soft grey blanket of dust,
Everything is just as it was.

A folded newspaper tells of an
Airline crash, the worst to date,
Thirty-seven people dead, no survivors.

I lean on the bench and scan the
Newspaper title, *The Daily Mail*,
February the tenth, Nineteen thirty-one.

Nothing has disturbed this accidental
Museum, a slice of industrial history
Frozen as a lifeless relic.

Sixty-two years have passed since
They abandoned this "Marie Celeste",
A ghost by the banks of the silent one.

TOPOGRAPHY SKETCHES

1.
Grey scars run over
The soft green skin,
Patiently waiting for
Mother Nature's healing kiss.

2.
Two blackfaced sheep
Lie sleeping in the fank,
Created by rain
On this 20th century tumulus.

3.
Opportunists now reside
On the steep earth banks,
Dried veins which once carried
The lifeblood of a new age.

4.
Rain slowly dissolves
The great red remains,
Washing them back into
The ground from which they came.

5.
White birk bones
Laid gravely in rows,
Once cool silver light
Reflected from your boughs.

6.
Jock dances through
The long deep cauldron,
Sings with rock and rowan
Of his marriage to Clotha.

7.
Standing proud
Five iron red bings,
Modern earthworks
Formed of ancient ore.

ALONE

Tom Crowe

The scene is a large kitchen. A long table stands alongside
a window through which the sunlight is streaming. A
woman sits at the head of the table, her face turned away
from the window, and in shadow. In front of her lies an
opened envelope and two pages of handwritten notepaper.
Near these are: a box of tissues, several unopened, typed
envelopes, a small dark bottle. The kitchen, though full of
smart modern equipment, looks shabby, with unwashed
crockery lying here and there. The woman looks towards
us. We see that she is about fifty, with quite strong
handsome features. She picks up the letter. She speaks, with
a slight northern accent.

"I got this from him a few days ago . . . no, of course it
wasn't . . . must have been almost two weeks ago. Anyway
—just like Ted! He never was able to talk about things! He
went off on this business trip down south—the company
were having some sort of trouble with the new factory
down there and Ted was going to sort it out—and then, a
few days later, this came through the door . . . ."

She pauses, looking down at the letter, turning the pages
over and over. She laughs, nervously, hopelessly.

"It *was* quite a shock. I hadn't a clue, really. Well,
everyone has their problems occasionally, don't they, but
you get over them, you go on. I didn't know things were this
bad. Not as bad as *he* says they were. To read this you
would think we'd been fighting like cats and dogs for the
last twenty years—well, *I* had been fighting—he reckons he
gave up ten years ago. And all this money he'd been

making, where's it all gone, he wants to know. And the way I'd brought up the children. And . . . ."

She turns her head away again, back into shadow.

". . . And the sex."

She looks at us again.

"Seems it was never much good. All these years—and it wasn't much good."

Her voice falters, her control breaks, just a little.

"That wasn't very nice, Ted Hewitt. You could have left that out."

She sighs.

"Yes, it's all in here. Amazing, isn't it? My life, all in a couple of pages . . . . These other letters have turned up since. I haven't opened them—they look like solicitors' letters to me. I haven't done much of anything since this came—me that used to be so, well . . . so proud of the way I kept the place. And look at it now."

She gazes around the kitchen, and we look too, at the littered worktops, the sink full of dirty plates and mugs, the stained cooker. She looks at us again.

"I'd never have let it go like this. But now I just can't be bothered. Ted came back, you know, yesterday I think it was. Just walked in—didn't knock or anything. He came in and stood there, at the door, looking round. I think he got a bit of a shock, seeing the place like this. Well! What am I supposed to do? He's away. The kids are away. We've got two floors of nothing here—nothing. Why should I . . . ?"

She looks down at the paper twisted between her fingers. She nods towards us.

"He sat down, just there, at the end of the table, and started to tell me what I should be doing—get a solicitor—get him to answer the letters—start thinking about the future. Oh, I can't remember all what he said—he went on and on. I do remember that at one point I said, 'Are you coming home, Ted?' Well, *that* stopped him in his tracks. 'I'm wasting my time here,' he said, 'you haven't been listening to a word I said.' And he got up and walked out. No word of regret, or comfort even, no attempt to justify himself, no goodbye. It was a bit like having a car accident —you know, when the two cars hit each other and it's the other person's fault and you know it but you know they're not going to admit anything even if they want to—it's just 'Insurance company details, please,' and off they go. Well, there I was, nursing some serious damage somewhere, and no insurance cover."

She smiles—a wan, tired smile.

"I suppose I should get the place cleaned up. It's shock, of course. Oh yes, I know *that* well enough. The doctor gave me some sleeping-pills . . . ."

She picks up the small brown bottle and pours a few tablets onto the table.

"Just a few. That was in case I decided to take the lot all at once. I should really tidy things up. I always used to keep the place so nice. The kids were always teasing me about it —like the time I finally got Ted to agree to new carpets— lovely pale green carpets, but then the only trouble was they'd show up the slightest mark. Well, I put notices up, here at this door into the hallway, and at the front door— 'NO BOOTS OR SHOES BEYOND HERE!'"

She emphasises the words, drawing an imaginary line under them in the air, and laughs quietly.

"Well, it was just a little habit of mine. Notices in the bathroom and the kids' bedrooms—'WASH YOUR HANDS'—'TIDY UP NOW!' They all teased me about it. The kids would say, 'What if our friends come round. Do we have to tell them to take their shoes off or to make sure

70

they flush the toilet?' Oh dear! the fuss they made! Anyway, there wasn't any problem—the kids went round to their friends and Ted and I usually met up with our friends in the local at the weekends. So the notices stayed up—and the carpets stayed clean! The whole place was clean. *And* I did it all myself."

She is silent for a moment, brooding over the past.

"Now *he* says I wore myself out over the place, and wore him out too. He says twenty years is more than enough and another five years would probably kill him and I'd be responsible. He says the kids are away and he doesn't love me any more, so what's the point?"

She scrabbles at the box of tissues and holds some to her eyes.

"He says he's just tired. Tired! Well, I've been tired—exhausted—but you carry on somehow, don't you? You don't just give up. He says there's no one else—but I know better. There'll be some young tart making up to him for a bit of fun and he's fallen for it like a ton of bricks. God, how stupid men can be!"

She presses her hands to her face for a moment, then looks up and smiles bravely.

"The kids have been good. They understand all right. They've phoned, oh, often. One of them will probably phone tonight."

She looks towards the telephone on the window-sill and half reaches out towards it.

"There's another woman all right. There has to be."

She looks around vaguely.

"I should really start clearing up."

But she doesn't move. She picks up the letter again. She turns her head away from the sunlight, back into the shadow.

71

POEMS

Paul Dawson

SOMETIMES . . . SADNESS

Sometimes I dream
I'm standing over the stump of a felled tree
looking and pointing
at
Summer and Winter,
each claustrophobic summer

Sometimes I have thoughts that I don't feel
but trouble me since I thought them
Burning like the Klansmen's cross
they leave charred wood and destruction

Sometimes happiness drips from me
like a leaky tap
Sometimes it falls
like the level of an emptying tank

Some thoughts turn their own soil
but others gnaw and tear at the edges
until
they finally drive the spade deep enough.

SEX

I'm doing it all the time—
on the box
while I'm sitting
while I stand

It's flashing through my head
and lying in my mind

Once it was under the covers
now it's under the eye
of some home moving
forward winding
slow
framed
mindscape
painter

It's worth more than the discussion we give it.

SHOPPING MAUL

"Surely we credit consumers
with common sense"

People slip past each other
as smoothly as in dance
With eyes wishing
through windows so big I see small
Riding escalators to
plunder new lands, sucking
surgically synthesised air
from hot-housed plants of a true green
colonised by sniggering invaders

. . . and mirrors reflect
and I see I'm for sale!
Marble floors as cold and hard
as the money that made them,
and water falls
whispering hypnotically
spend spend spend,
and never ending piano music
wallpapers the walls
as the sun ripens my temper.

APRIL

We stood, my friends and I
We stood in the middle of the bar
rattling the ice in our drinks
She glanced over, smiling
We sat at an empty table
Smiling, she clambered over,
standing on a seat
and my jacket,
before sitting

She talked to me
I mean, she talked to me

When she was younger, about nineteen
she met a guy. He was Italian
Quite charming, and made her laugh
He walked her home
They went out together for a while
He took her, and left a kid
Catholic and confused and scared
she had an abortion
Confided in her sister, who crucified her soul
She had pain so deep it was her

We sat together with nothing and nobody around
Her eyes held tears
My eyes held them too
I told her what I knew
and had just discovered
But it wasn't enough
April, if you can listen
Forgive me
What the hell do I know.

THE FISHERMEN

Cigarettes burn aglow,
dancing like fireflies in the night
Erratic movements follow gestures of thought—
betraying more than the tongue lets slip
A forced respiration—a warning sign,
and clouds of smoke diffuse in silence
The smoke is black like their lungs and
thick like their skin

A bottle is tossed,
and arcs, whistling to itself
Neck above water, its lungs slowly fill,
until,
with a gurgled last it looses the bonds
No mark made
No measure of existence

Quiet, though never still
the water forms a noose around beams of wood
Thrust into the water
and secured to last, a common past
Old wood laps old water;
while the new stands strong
and erect
and unshaken

A life hard
but lived true
where unhurried widows
weep the dew.

THE ROOM

Agnes Thomson

There was a room in her grandmother's house which Beth feared and hated, or perhaps the room hated Beth, the noisy intruder.

The room was no longer in use, a door to be hurried past on dark winter evenings, especially when it stood ajar. But it held a lure which drew Beth inside time after time. There she would stay, enraptured, until a chill would settle around her shoulders, and the half-remembered, old man smell would fill her nostrils and she would be forced to flee, feet scattering the rugs on the polished linoleum, hands slithering on the smooth, round, wooden doorknob. Only when she had crossed the threshold would she dare to sneak her hand back inside to flick off the light switch, tensing herself against the unseen touch which never came. Then she would scurry towards the light glowing at the end of the gloomy passageway—to the kitchen—and safety. Until the next time.

The room had belonged to Beth's great uncle. She couldn't understand why she should be so frightened of being there alone—Uncle Joe had never harmed her when he was alive. Looking back years later, she wondered if she avoided spending too much time there in case she might somehow absorb the essence of the man he had been, and in some way tempt the same fate.

"Oor Joe was a gey clever man," Beth's grandmother often remarked sadly.

By all accounts, he had been an extremely clever man, but the darkness of a boyhood and manhood spent down the pit had extinguished any ambitions he may have cherished. Great Uncle Joe had crossed the fine line before he died.

He had never been inside a church in his life, but Uncle Joe studied his bible assiduously. His debates with the "Holy Willie" side of the family were legendary. He parried their thrusting quotes with those of his own, until they retreated almost purple-faced with frustration. The local teacher often visited him in his later years to debate and set the world to rights. He could argue politics, religion and science with anyone who dared to take him on. He had been a fine artist. His oil paintings were the only bright spot among the heavy furniture of his room. They remained there after his death, a visual epitaph to his talent.

In one corner of his room stood another reminder of Joe's gifts, and it was this that brought Beth into the room as often as she dared. It was a large organ with pedals which dwarfed her feet, and several interesting wooden stops inlaid with mother-of-pearl. While Beth pretended to play the organ, her imagination soared. She entertained vast audiences and was applauded rapturously. Then the memory of Uncle Joe would invade her daydreams and force her to seek the company of the rest of her family.

Her grandmother's house was the meeting place of a large but close-knit family. They gathered there to talk and laugh and celebrate, to be close. Beth loved the times when the house was full of her relatives, for then she had various cousins to play with. Hogmanay was especially exciting. Then, the house would be full to bursting point, not only with the family, but also friends and neighbours, as the adults celebrated the birth of a new year with hope in their hearts, while the children were satisfied with the joy of being allowed to stay up so late.

At other times, Beth was the only child in the house. She didn't mind this, for she could spend hours listening to the adults' conversation without being bored. She learned her family history by keeping her ears open and her mouth shut.

Beth had a favourite hiding place in the living-room, under the chenille-covered wooden table. It was, at times, her house, where she played with her dolls, at times a dark and mysterious cave full of treasures and sometimes a covered wagon, drawn by a team of fine white horses, as Beth escaped from the savage Red Indians, dodging their arrows and firing her rifle with perfect precision.

It was here that Beth first learned what was going to happen to Uncle Joe.

"I cannae cope any longer," her grandmother cried. "I nursed oor mother until she died, but this is different. I never ken whit he's goin' tae dae next."

"But Grace, he's oor brother, we cannae dae that tae him!"

"Then you take him, Davie, or you, Andra, for I've done ma bit and noo I need a rest. The strain is too much for me at my age."

There were no offers of help and Uncle Joe's fate was decided.

Beth had realised that something had gone wrong with him, but was too young to know what the problem was.

Except for explosive bursts of temper, he hardly spoke. He stopped going outside and had begun to pace from one side of the living-room to the other, as if a route had been set out for him from which he dare not deviate. He began to show violent tendencies towards Beth's grandmother.

One day, from under the table, Beth watched as the two men led him away. With one man holding each elbow he twisted his head round, his eyes glassy.

"Grace?" he pleaded.

Beth watched as her grandmother hung her head and turned away. She never saw Uncle Joe again.

His room remained unchanged, a cold square in a warm house.

Robert Hume

The coming rain smudged Tinto to a green blur;
Cold grey duvets slowly tucking down,
Their low silence
Punctuated by the wipers' scrape.
Droplets spattered the screen, then gathered—maybe
    over the hill—
For the next wind-driven assault.

Over the bend and down the hill,
Waiting, ruby monocle on a rusty tripod.
CAUTION. RESURFACING WORK.
In the distance, hard-hatted functionaries:
The young, laughing slack-mouthed
At their sudden power; older sweats
Idling, not meeting the eye,
Waiting for place and time to meet
In synchronised task.
And around all the steam, the thumping compressor,
The sticky odour of tar.

Over the field's heaving hill,
As if summoned, the tractor bounced.
Gleam of white, chrome verticals;
Radiator looming, rim of hard azure.
All heads turned at its clanking grandeur,
Following the slow curves as segs of mud
Gouted from the tyres' dinosaur tread.

Above the fence, the boy drops down.
New boots, new boilersuit: navy, gleaming studs,
    trouser rolls.

Walks slowly; inhales our stares; looks overlong
At the counterweights: too black, neatly stacked.
Then back to the bucket, hefts the
Creosoted posts, the linseed-shafted mell,
Sword, spears against the road's rampart.

Ahead, the light winks to green.
Heads slowly turn to the road's compulsion,
Steering-wheels flex, pedals wait to pump.

The boy pats the head of the first broken post,
And circles to leap.
His arc tangles on the barbed wire teeth, is caught,
For a moment tented by it.
Then he slides, slithers, rights himself.
Hand over inside of thigh
He looks back—at us, then the tractor.
No-one wants to see the dull red
On his fingers, the brighter flush spreading
From the raw cheekbones.
As we slid on to our own fences, our own repairs,
No one grudged the chrome handles, the black grille
Misting now as the air wept
At hills and clouds fusing together, moving in.

THRESHOLDS

How strange: the word tailing, "You're . . ."
The slamming echoes in retreating footsteps, the hissing
Of the gas fire; further supply of the missing words
Cut off by the still quivering door.
So different from our usual posts: "Who
Do you think you are?" etched down one jamb. Hovering
Over that handle—cracked fifties bakelite—covered
By white fingers, "Just once, just once, you
Might apologise." While my hands, red
And clumsy, pause mid thigh, echo the slide
Of shoulders towards rooted feet. Perhaps later
The right words will come. Yet after, outside
Some other threshold; "You don't like doors, do you?"
    she said.
My feet falter, unsure, wary of exchanging one room
    for another.

HAWK

And then, suddenly, their heads arched downwards.
"Look! A hawk!" Inevitably, so it was,
Steepling on the top curve of the windscreen glass,
Twining tighter the rigging between road
And verge and cloud.
As ever, the head with the comma's
Blunt stillness, hooked; the blackness
Blurred by whirring wings, tied
To its target. And then dropping, like death,
Go the years so I see once again
My father, treed, lopping saw in hand,
Open-mouthed as the sparrowhawk grazed his branch.
Stopping the goldfinch's heart. Settling in their seats,
My children turn ahead, see only the road's wide,
    unravelling straightness.

83

DEAD BIRDS

I

Blackbird,
But feathers mud brown,
Dead.
Wings shrug against the ground below
Sidelong
Eyes squinting, Egyptian, over the beak
Glued to the tarmac of the road.
But, as if tickled by the gravel, hips look
To twitch, splay-footed and ridiculous, into dance-step.

II

And twenty paces further,
The wide road narrowing to a rutted lane,
But clearly—from the sky—an
Aerodrome; dew on
Jewelled hedges making a failed flightpath
For this crashlanding.
Wings out, wide, on a tired dihedral.
Undercarriage? Well, probably down.
But no head.
No pilot.

III

Round the corner it was.
First morning of an early, false spring;
The morning torn between a melting dampness
And the tight grip of the winter sun.
That bright sun, so its eyes closed
Tight over the moment of death;

Concentration rather than repose.
Plumage fluffy over the breast, yet
Already rat-tailing towards the thighs.
Colour and size of a finch,
But the beak all wrong, too sharp.
And it lay there, perchless but perched,
Claws grasping, still, at the invisible.
Looking round, there was no branch, no cable,
No possible arc for its falling.
Nothing save the puddles' refracted flashes
Measuring the sun's declension.

IV

Spring. Traffic racing towards the junction, speeding
    into sudden stops.
Two blackbirds, chasing the fizzing orange tracers
    of their beaks,
Under hedges, between cast-iron stanchions. Narrow,
    busy loops
Skimming the tarmac sticky black against the
    morning's pale texture,
Flicking the leaves, leaving black after-shapes
On the eyes' soft pathways. Then, seeking
The ultimate twin parabola,
One twist, pike and loop too far
Leaving one unstitched black carpet, claw upward.
What memories? Brake lines for branches, the heat
    of the exhaust?
What of the other? Its curves loosening, eventually
Straightening on a path to elsewhere.
And which remained? Pursuer or pursued?
Against the grinding tyres the claw remains,
Stretching, clutching
Towards definition.

BUT IT WON'T EVER HAPPEN

Ian Hunter

"Have you ever thought of setting your stories in England?"

Writer flinches with surprise, Redland thought, leaning back in his chair. "Why would I do that?"

"You might sell more books?"

The author nodded slowly. "No one's ever suggested that, but it's not something I would do anyway. Write from what you know. That's one of the first rules of writing. And I know Scotland, or at least certain parts of it. If I set something in . . . the Lake District, for example, it would probably be about a Scot visiting Windermere and getting involved in something horrible. But why bother? Our country is rich enough in myth and history and culture to provide endless ideas for horror stories."

"But your latest novel isn't a horror novel," the librarian next to him pointed out.

Never one to miss an opportunity, Redland held up *The Writers' Group* in front of the small audience gathered in the library. "Only £9.99," he said. "Hurry now while stocks last."

As soon as the laughter died a man in the front row said, "Why is it so cheap? Is it because you're afraid of disappointing your usual readers?"

Redland smiled, it wasn't a new question. "No, I want to give my readers value for money, and while I think this is the greatest thing since sliced bread, it's still only two hundred pages long, so why charge £14.99 for a copy?"

A young woman leaned forward, cocked her head to the side, held up her hand tentatively, then finally asked, "Are you disappointed with the reviews so far?"

Redland waved his hand dismissively in what he hoped was a "who cares" gesture.

"At least I'm getting reviewed with this one," he pointed out. "Reviews of my horror novels are rare in Scotland, unless they're in the 'worst of the year' category."

"You sound bitter," a man remarked.

"Yes and no," the writer admitted. "A lot of getting published is down to luck. Who you know. Which circles you mix in, or belong to. Scottish writing is supposed to be angry. On the edge, where many of the writers are financially. You suffer for your art. Well fuck suffering. I'll take the money any time."

The librarian coughed.

Redland held up his hand. "Pardon the French, but I think it's true. I write to make money. To be famous. I'm not Stephen King, but I make a living, and a lot of that living comes from other parts of the world. From people with preconceived ideas about Scotland created by watching films like *Lassie Come Home* and *Local Hero*. They don't want to read about homelessness and unemployment and the fight for a Scottish voice. They want to escape, and that's what I provide, escapism. From terrible lifestyles and the real horror that goes on in the world."

"But your books are pretty gory," said someone in the second row.

Wagging a finger, Redland nodded. "Yes, but still escapism. People get killed in my books in quite gruesome and spectacular ways, I admit that. Some of my friends are doctors and firemen, and a great source of information, but what I write about won't ever happen in real life. My deaths are too elaborate. I provide entertainment, that's all."

He glanced at his watch. Time was marching on. He had promised the guys he would visit the group, just like old times. He looked at the audience. Some of them had bought copies of *The Writers' Group* from the library. Others had brought one or two of his horror novels, and a few sat with carrier bags on their knees. Hopefully not with manuscripts inside.

"Does anyone have a final question?" the librarian asked.

A few people put up their hands, but one man shouted, "How do you get published?"

"By writing," Redland told him. "That's the only way. By writing every day and sending your work out, and getting plenty of rejections. Some of which will arrive within days or weeks and make you wonder if they ever read your stuff, while others will take months and months and make you wonder if they ever got it, or even worse, if they are ripping you off. But keep writing. I've met too many people who want to be rich and famous writers, but they never write. They expect to wake up one morning and find the typewriter fairies have been at work and there's a complete manuscript on their desk. Which they will send off and immediately get accepted, and the book will be published the following week, ripping through the bestseller lists before being made into a box-office smash that will make them even more rich and famous."

"Sounds easy," the man replied, and everyone laughed, then applauded on the prompting of the librarian.

A photographer from the local rag bullied them to stand around Redland with cheesy grins on their faces and copies of *The Writers' Group* in their hands.

And at that moment Redland didn't care if they hadn't all bought a copy. He was lovingly stroking the cover of the novel as if it was alive, and it was, to him. Bursting with energy. Big. Ballsy. Taking no prisoners. Full of meaty prose that didn't give a damn. This was writer as god with all the excesses that implied. Some people might be able to take or leave it, but they couldn't ignore it.

He nodded, shook several hands and muttered thanks for coming, again and again, all the time aware of a youth lingering outside the library. One of mine, he wondered. Too shy to come inside? Probably not. Just a kid waiting for his date to arrive.

Another glance at his watch told him his old group would be meeting in fifteen minutes. He felt nervous, and sipped some wine, and still managed to look amiable despite the sour taste in his mouth. Typical council function. No major expense incurred. It would be better in the back room of The King's Tavern with a pint in his hand and a few old buddies looking at him with awe. God, he hoped they hadn't brought their manuscripts with them. Take a look at this, Tom, would you? Maybe you know an agent, or a publisher.

Though there were worse things than people wanting favours. Over the years he had sent the group a copy of his novels, all paperback originals to add to the small library they kept of their successes. Mostly small press stuff, or the odd appearance in one of the few Scottish mainstream magazines. But he hadn't sent them *The Writers' Group* for obvious reasons, the chief one being they were in it. The names were changed as were occupations and circumstances. But they were still there. Write from what you know, he had said, and he knew about writers' groups. Starting with being a member of one in his home town, then joining a few more in Glasgow, a couple in Edinburgh, before the six-month long nightmare of running a group in Drumchapel, where his major achievement had been to stay in one piece, and not become embroiled in serious crime. After that he had vowed never to take another group again, but that didn't stop him writing about an imaginary one, peopled from the collection of dreamers, winners, losers, perverts, egomaniacs, liars and crooks he had met down the years.

He thanked the librarian and let himself out of the building. Morrison's bookshop was across the street. An old family business where he had bought DC and Marvel comics displayed in a rusty revolving stand that said AMERICAN COMICS at the top. When he was older he had bought sheet music for his guitar at another stand. Looking in the window it seemed they sold neither these days, but at least his books were arranged in columns with a smiling photograph on top, and a notice:

> LOCAL AUTHOR
> TOM REDLAND
> SIGNING HERE
> TUESDAY 17TH
> 2pm

Which was tomorrow, and scanning the window he noticed that someone called John Dunlop was coming next week to promote copies of his book *Oil and Ecology Don't Mix*, about the Shetland oil disaster.

"Mr Redland?"

He looked round. So he had been right. The kid was one of his. Digging into a green M & S bag and pulling out copies of his horror novels like a magician. Two, three editions of the same title, some in American import. When he had finished there was a pile of books under his chin.

"I'm sorry," said Redland, "I don't have time to sign all those."

"But I've waited all night," the youth complained.

"You could have come into the library."

"No." The eyes looking at Redland turned hard. "The Dragon Lady hates horror novels."

"Who?"

"The librarian."

Redland shrugged. "She seemed pleasant enough."

"She would, with an adult, and some free booze."

"Look, I really don't have the time. Can't you come to Morrison's tomorrow?"

"No, I'm at school."

"Okay, give me one of each title, and I'll sign them. Fair enough?"

"I suppose so."

"What's your name?"

"Martin."

Redland took one copy of *Vampire Blues*, *Haunted Heart*, *Blood Zone*, *The Crawlers* and *Out of the Earth* and dedicated each to Martin, adding "Good luck with the Dragon" in the last.

Martin held his bag open and Redland slipped them inside. Then he saw the hardback.

"What's that?"

"Your latest."

"I'll sign it if you want."

Martin shook his head, his face looked twisted, sour. "No, don't bother."

"Why? Don't you like it?"

The youth snorted. "It's rubbish."

91

So much for holding back. Redland managed to force a smile. "Oh, really?"

"Definitely."

"Well, I'm glad you think so."

"You should stick to horror."

"Thanks for the tip," Redland said dryly, trying to ignore the doubt that was beginning to rise inside him. He couldn't make his mind up if Martin was making a valid point, or was just disappointed because he didn't get all his books signed. Would all his readers feel this way? Suddenly doubt gave way to depression, fuelled by the feeling that few people would read his book. He had created his own Catch-22. His normal readership wouldn't like his latest novel, and no one else would bother because he was pigeon-holed as a horror writer.

"Except you should keep it all the same. *Haunted Heart* isn't scary enough."

Suddenly the anger was back. "Oh, like *The Writers' Group*, you mean? If you must know *Haunted Heart* is a ghost story not a horror story."

Martin shuffled on his feet. "At least it's not a rip-off."

"Neither is this!"

There was a sneer on the boy's face. "Your other books sound real, like they could happen, but this . . ." He pulled the hardback out of the bag. ". . . is full of really unreal people and situations."

"But they are real."

"I don't believe you."

Redland waved his hand. "Then don't. What would you know anyway?"

"I know it's a rip-off, don't I? £9.99. I'll bet you'll charge £4.99 for the paperback."

God, talk about a dissatisfied customer, Redland thought.

He didn't have the time to explain about the price of a book, and who got their cuts, and how little was left for him. "Well, it was nice speaking to you," he said, and almost winced. What a dumb thing to say, but he was running on automatic from a thousand other encounters. "I have to get going."

Martin held out *The Writers' Group*.

"Here, you take it."

"Don't you want it?"

"It's crap."

"Look, son, piss off. I'm not in the mood for this."

"Fuck you," Martin snarled, and tore the book in two.

Redland's hand jerked up. "No, you can't—" What? What was he going to say? No, you can't rip it up? Well, too late. His big, ballsy pride and joy had just been castrated.

Martin turned and stomped down the street. He raised an arm, then dropped it, hard, spiking the halves of the novel into a litter-bin, as if scoring at basketball.

Redland closed his eyes.

Everything went black.

When he opened them again, the world seemed different. Then he realised there were little glowing lights in his vision, wriggling like luminous worms caused by an increase of pressure on his eyeballs. He reached up to his throat and checked the pulse in his neck. It seemed normal. He wasn't going to have a heart attack after all, despite the shock of seeing his breakthrough novel being ripped to pieces in front of him.

He hesitated, wanting to reclaim the remains from the bin. Stuff it, he thought, that would just be giving in to Martin and his opinions. What did he know anyway? He was just a kid.

Hands in pockets he marched towards the pub. The first thing he noticed when he entered was noise, then the heat, which caused his glasses to steam up immediately. He took them off and wiped the lenses with his thumbs. A TV was playing high on a shelf in the corner, but no one could hear it above the thump, thump of the jukebox.

He went to the bar. The barman smiled at him.

"Hi, Tom, what'll it be? The usual?"

"Thanks," Redland said hesitantly, while desperately trying to remember if he knew the man. It had been years since he had last been in the Tavern. Could this have been the barman then? Of course not, he was too young, Redland decided.

"Lager-tops," said the barman, placing the pint on a bar towel.

"Great," said Redland, handing over two pound coins, and waited for his change.

The barman dropped some silver into his hand. "Cheers, Tom, how's your dad?"

Redland's mouth opened, but no sound came out. He swallowed, and thought he must have misheard. It was still a painful subject, even after this time. His father had died five years earlier, the victim of a series of strokes. Redland had missed it all, too busy in America where *The Crawlers* was up for a Stoker Award. It didn't win, and by the time he made it back his father was dead. Gone forever. If only he had left the convention when he heard about the first stroke. Caught a flight back to Glasgow. He might have made it in time.

The barman nodded and turned away to serve someone else.

Redland looked around the pub. He couldn't see any of the old crowd. He checked his watch. The writers' group would soon be starting upstairs. Holding his pint tight he began to squeeze past the customers.

The wallpaper on the staircase had changed, and caricatures in pine frames hung on the walls. Billy Connolly, Sean Connery, Ally McCoist. On and on, up the stairs. At the top he could hear voices beyond the door at the end of the corridor. He knocked and entered. The room hadn't changed at all. Even the air seemed to crackle with tales of the latest submissions, rejections and acceptances.

"Hi, Tom."

Redland smiled. It was Andy Smith standing beside the kettle. He looked round. Jim Prentice and Dan Forsyth sat at the table along with three others he didn't recognise.

"Coffee?" asked Andy.

Redland held up his pint. "No, thanks." He walked around the table and glanced at the bookcase filled with guides to writing and copies of magazines that had published stories or poems by members of the group. He couldn't see his own books, but they had probably been put aside for a signing session later.

He sat down at the head of the table.

One of the faces he didn't know frowned at him.

"What are you doing, Tom?"

"I'm sitting down."

"But that seat's for the guest writer."

"So?"

The man looked at his watch. "So, he'll be here any minute now."

Redland grinned. "Who?"

"John Dunlop, the ecology fellow."

"Isn't he coming next week? I saw something in Morrison's window that—"

"He's signing there tomorrow."

Redland laughed, and pointed to his chest. "I'm signing at Morrison's tomorrow."

The members of the writers' group looked at each other.

"What are you talking about, Tom?" asked Andy.

Redland slowly lowered his hand to the table and tapped it lightly. "Look, a joke's a joke, but this isn't the way to treat someone you haven't seen for years."

Dan stared at him. "Years? But you were here last week."

"Oh, really?"

"Sure, you read some horror stuff called 'The Creepers'."

"'The Crawlers'," Andy corrected.

Redland drummed his fingers off the table. "Right, the novel that was nominated for the Bram Stoker Award."

Jim laughed. "Did it win?"

"No."

Andy stirred his coffee. "And when did all this happen, Tom?"

"Five years ago, when my father had his strokes."

Dan nodded. "Those were bad times."

"The worst," agreed Redland.

"But at least he didn't die, right?"

Redland glared at Dan. "Of course he died, you sick asshole!"

"Hey, watch your language, Tom, there's no need for that."

"My father is dead," Redland whispered, and looked around at six faces which seemed concerned, and puzzled, and a little pissed off.

"But I saw him last Tuesday," Andy said. "He was—"

"You did not!"

Suddenly the door opened, and a man entered carrying

96

a large travel bag. "Hello, I'm John Dunlop."

Jim leaned forward. "You better move, Tom, that seat is for the guest writer."

"Oh, I'll move all right," Redland muttered, standing up. "Hello, I'm Tom Redland, the horror writer. I used to be a member of this group."

"Really?" said Dunlop, shaking hands.

"No," said Andy. "Tom's just having you on."

"I am not." Redland looked at Dunlop. "You've heard of me, haven't you?"

"I'm afraid not."

"But you must have, I'm a famous horror writer."

"Sorry. I don't read that sort of thing. There's enough horror in the real world. Take my book," said Dunlop, swinging his bag on to the table. "I'm signing copies at Morrison's tomorrow, and—"

"No, I'm doing that!"

The hand on Redland's shoulder made him jerk. He looked round. "Enough, Tom, you're making a fool of yourself and the group."

Redland pulled away. "No, I'm a writer. I've had six novels published and received two award nominations."

"Put another record on," said one of the members he didn't know.

Redland pointed at him. "I'll prove what I'm saying. I'll show you."

He ran downstairs and through the pub, and had almost reached the door when a voice stopped him.

"Hey, Tommy!"

Only one person had ever called him Tommy. No, thought Redland. No. It couldn't be. He didn't want to turn, because he knew that corner of the pub. Where the old men always sat, his father among them, playing dominoes

97

and chewing over the past.

He really didn't want to turn.

His father smiled at him, and raised his walking-stick, then turned his attention back to the dominoes spread out across his large palm.

Redland barged through the group of people next to the door and almost fell into the street. This was all wrong, all of it. He was the victim of a cruel hoax. Imagine getting someone to play his father. The sick bastards. God, they must really envy him, must really hate him to go to such lengths. But suppose it was true. Suppose he was mad, believing all of this. His father dead. His fame. His other life as a writer.

My real life, he told himself, and slapped his hand against his thigh. He would have the last laugh. He could prove he was a writer.

He ran down the street to the litter-bin and searched for the copy of *The Writers' Group*, but it wasn't there.

The boy came back for it, he thought, because I'm his favourite writer. He would probably turn up at Morrison's tomorrow with the book held together by sellotape, and sheepishly ask for an autograph.

He crossed the street and nodded to himself, convinced that would happen, and looked in the bookshop window.

> SCOTTISH AUTHOR
> JOHN DUNLOP
> SIGNING HERE
> TUESDAY 17TH
> 2pm

A smiling picture of Dunlop sat on top of a pile of books. Yes, thought Redland, that's the same man. Appearing here. Tomorrow. Instead of me.

He closed his eyes and leaned against the window. He turned his cheek against the glass. It felt cool and forgiving. He hoped when he opened his eyes he would be a famous writer again, but he wasn't ready to open them, not just yet.